Sumatran Tigers

Sumatran Tigers

Guardians of the Rainforest

Sanyub S.

UNIEK ENTERPRISES

CONTENTS

INDEX

5.2Discussion on the involvement of local communities, NGOs, and governmental organizations in these efforts.

Chapter 6 Challenges and Solutions

6.1Identification and analysis of the challenges faced by conservationists in safe-guarding Sumatran tigers.

6.2Exploration of innovative solutions and strategies to overcome these challenges.

Chapter 7Success Stories

7.1Spotlight on successful case studies and examples of conservation efforts that have positively impacted Sumatran tiger populations.

7.2Inspiration for future conservation endeavors.

Chapter 8The Future of Sumatran Tigers

8.1Examination of the long-term prospects for Sumatran tigers.

8.2Discussion on the importance of continued conservation efforts and the role of global collaboration.

Chapter 9 Conclusion

9.1Recapitulation of the unique status and importance of Sumatran tigers.

9.2Call to action for readers to contribute to the conservation of these magnificent creatures and their rainforest habitat.

The emerald-toned rainforests of Sumatra, an Indonesian gem settled in the western spans of the archipelago, have long enamored the creative mind of naturalists and experience searchers the same. Inside this lavish and biodiverse material, one superb animal stands as an image of the sensitive equilibrium that supports life in this rich environment — the Sumatran tiger (Panthera tigris sumatrae). In the accompanying investigation, we set out on a broad excursion through the multifaceted woven artwork of the Sumatran tiger's presence, unwinding the strings that wind around together its biological importance, the horde dangers it defies, and the enthusiastic protection endeavors pointed toward saving this famous species.

The Verifiable Epic of Sumatran Tigers

The Sumatran tiger, a particular subspecies of its catlike genealogy, has not only slinked through the pages of history but rather has recorded its story into the actual texture of Sumatran culture. Here, in the old legends, old stories, and customs of neighborhood networks, the tiger possesses a worshipped and on occasion, a dreaded space. Its presence has been weaved with profound imagery, epitomizing both the cryptic appeal of the wild and the potential peril hiding inside the thick shadows of the rainforest.

In investigating the authentic elements of Sumatran tigers, we dive into the account of conjunction among people and these radiant animals. The tiger, when an undisputed ruler of the Sumatran wildernesses, presently explores a world changed by human exercises. As we follow the strides of this dominant hunter through the archives of time, we uncover the advancing connection between Sumatran tigers and the native networks that share their environment.

Biological Orchestra of Sumatran Tigers

Past their lofty appearance and the rush they bring out, Sumatran tigers play out an imperative job in the complex orchestra of the rainforest. As dominant hunters, they organize the fragile equilibrium of the biological system, directing prey populaces and forestalling unrestrained development that could prompt the corruption of the climate. Their presence, a demonstration of the biological strength of the rainforest, resounds through the interconnected trap of life that depends on their guardianship.

To comprehend the natural meaning of Sumatran tigers, we adventure into the core of their living space. The rainforest, abounding with assorted vegetation, wakes up from the perspective of tiger environment. We investigate the nuanced connections among tigers and their prey, the effect of their presence on vegetation, and the flowing impacts that resonate through each layer of the environment.

Besides, the Sumatran tiger turns into a pointer species, a litmus test for the general soundness of the rainforest. Their downfall, intelligent of natural surroundings misfortune and corruption, sends swells through the scene, flagging a looming emergency that reaches out past the destiny of a solitary animal types. In this part, we unwind the complicated dance of life that relies on the endurance of Sumatran tigers.

Confronting Shadows - Dangers to Sumatran Tigers

The once-unassailable rule of Sumatran tigers faces an existential danger, creating inauspicious shaded areas over the rainforest's most notable occupants. The essential bad guy in this unfurling show is human movement, creating a long shaded area that stretches across the delicate environments of Sumatra. Natural surroundings misfortune, the tireless juggernaut of deforestation driven by farming, logging, and foundation advancement, arises as the key impetus behind the tigers' decay.

As tractors cut through the tribal domains of Sumatran tigers, the actual groundworks of their reality disintegrate. The once touching spans of rainforest contract, leaving the tigers segregated and powerless. Discontinuity not just disturbs the normal ways of behaving of these animals yet additionally intensifies the dangers they face. Hereditary variety, a key part for the drawn out endurance of any species, wanes as detachment sets in, further risking the Sumatran tiger populace.

The infringement of human settlements onto conventional tiger regions compounds the difficulties. Human-natural life clashes heighten, driven by rivalry for assets and space. The gatekeepers of the rainforest wind up entrapped in a snare of contentions, where the outcomes of endurance frequently conflict with the requirements of extending human populaces.

Poaching, a troubling phantom tormenting the universe of untamed life preservation, arises as another imposing danger. Driven by the guileful requests of the unlawful untamed life exchange, Sumatran tigers succumb to the unquenchable hunger for their bones, skin, and other body parts. Conventional drugs, intriguing pets, and decorative things fuel this illegal exchange, leaving the tiger populace near the precarious edge of destruction.

Environmental change, an overall test of our times, adds a layer of intricacy to the situation of Sumatran tigers. Modified weather conditions, moving prey accessibility, and the more extensive effects of a changing environment make an extra arrangement of difficulties for these strong animals. As the environment emergency strengthens, the gatekeepers of the rainforest explore an undeniably questionable future.

Protection Narratives - Beams of Trust

Despite difficulty, a partner of devoted traditionalists and associations arises as the vanguard, standing relentless in their obligation to safeguarding Sumatran tigers and the biological systems they call home. This section disentangles the multifaceted embroidery of protection endeavors, laying out a picture of trust in the midst of the shadows that take steps to immerse these glorious animals.

Safeguarded regions and untamed life saves arise as safe-havens where the gate-keepers of the rainforest can wander undisturbed. These protection strongholds act as essential fortifications, saving the normal ways of behaving and environmental jobs of Sumatran tigers. Endeavors to lay out and extend these safeguarded scenes represent an aggregate obligation to getting the fate of these famous animals.

Worldwide coordinated efforts and associations become key parts in the preservation story. Recognizing that the destiny of Sumatran tigers rises above public limits, protection associations, legislative bodies, and neighborhood networks join in shared liability. Together, they explore the complicated trap of political, social, and natural difficulties, making progress toward an agreeable concurrence that safeguards the trustworthiness of the rainforest.

Local area commitment becomes the dominant focal point in the preservation adventure. Perceiving the interlaced predeterminations of neighborhood networks and Sumatran tigers, drives center around encouraging practical vocations that lighten pressures on the rainforest. By coordinating nearby information and viewpoints, progressives enable networks to become dynamic members in the guardianship of their regular legacy.

Inventive mechanical arrangements carry another aspect to Sumatran tiger protection. From camera traps catching slippery minutes in the existence of a tiger to satellite observing giving bits of knowledge into development designs, innovation turns into an impressive partner in the battle against termination. The marriage of science and development opens new boondocks for understanding and safeguarding these baffling animals.

Training and mindfulness crusades become mobilizing cries in the worldwide work to save Sumatran tigers. By dispersing information about the environmental significance of these dominant hunters and the dangers they face, protectionists look to motivate aggregate activity. As the quiet thunder of Sumatran tigers resonates across the globe, a developing melody of voices joins the call for change.

An Ensemble Incomplete - The Eventual fate of Sumatran Tigers

As we close our odyssey through the rainforests of Sumatra and the existences of its gatekeepers, the fate of Sumatran tigers remains at a junction.

The story unfurls as an orchestra, with each note addressing a decision, a choice that reverberations through time. The watchmen of the rainforest, once undermined by shadows, coax humankind to assume a critical part in forming the fate of these great animals.

In thinking about the eventual fate of Sumatran tigers, we face basic inquiries. Might mankind at any point adapt to the situation of coinciding with these gatekeepers of the rainforest? Will the protection endeavors framed in these pages demonstrate adequate to switch the tide of dangers confronting Sumatran tigers? What heritage will we leave for people in the future, and will it incorporate the resonating thunder of Sumatran tigers reverberating through the emerald profundities of the rainforest?

The ensemble of the Sumatran tiger's presence stays incomplete, and the cudgel is in our grasp. Our decisions today will reverberate through the ages, deciding if these gatekeepers of the rainforest will keep on meandering openly or blur into the shadows of eradication. The source of inspiration is clear, enticing us to become stewards of an inheritance that rises above lines, societies, and time — a heritage where Sumatran tigers, as gatekeepers of the rainforest, stand as meaningful images of our obligation to an amicable conjunction with nature.

1. **Brief overview of the significance of Sumatran tigers in the ecosystem.**

   The lavish rainforests of Sumatra, hung in an emerald embroidery, harbor a large number of mysteries and stories. Among its numerous occupants, the Sumatran tiger (Panthera tigris sumatrae) arises as a cornerstone animal varieties, a gatekeeper of biodiversity complicatedly woven into the biological texture. In this complete investigation, we dive into the multi-layered meaning of Sumatran tigers in the biological system, disentangling their jobs as dominant hunters, natural controllers, and marks of ecological wellbeing.

   The Dominant hunters

   At the zenith of the pecking order, Sumatran tigers order a place of unmatched importance in the many-sided dance of hunter and prey. Their job as top hunters isn't just a demonstration of their solidarity and ability however a key power molding the elements of the whole biological system.

   Sumatran tigers fundamentally go after ungulates like deer and wild pig. This predation applies an immediate impact on the populace elements of these herbivores, forestalling unrestrained development that could prompt overgrazing and exhaustion of vegetation. By directing the quantities of herbivores, tigers in a roundabout way impact the piece and construction of plant networks, cultivating biodiversity.

   Besides, the simple presence of dominant hunters like the Sumatran tiger affects the way of behaving of prey species. Herbivores adjust by modifying their searching examples and staying away from high-risk regions visited by tigers. This social reaction not just improves the endurance impulses of prey species yet additionally adds to the upkeep of a reasonable and strong environment.

   Gatekeepers of Biodiversity

   Past their immediate effect on prey populaces, Sumatran tigers act as gatekeepers of biodiversity by keeping up with the trustworthiness of the environments they occupy. The idea of biodiversity includes the range of species as well as the hereditary variety inside populaces and the variety of biological systems themselves. In this specific circumstance, the job of dominant hunters in protecting biodiversity becomes vital.

Sumatran tigers add to biodiversity by forestalling the strength of a solitary animal types inside the biological system. Through their guideline of prey populaces, they make conditions that permit a huge number of plant and creature species to coincide. This natural congruity, molded by the presence of dominant hunters, brings about a mosaic of environments that upholds a different exhibit of life.

The soundness of environments is much of the time estimated by their biodiversity, and the decay of dominant hunters can set off a chain response prompting the unwinding of this perplexing web. On account of Sumatran tigers, their diminishing numbers signal a danger to their own reality as well as a potential disentangling of the different environments they help support.

Marks of Biological system Wellbeing

Sumatran tigers, with their subtle presence and finely tuned variations, arise as pivotal signs of the general soundness of the environments they possess. Their downfall or vanishing can act as an early advance notice framework, flagging aggravations or irregular characteristics inside the more extensive climate.

The wellbeing of Sumatran tiger populaces is unpredictably connected to the accessibility and nature of their environment. As commit carnivores, these tigers depend on solid populaces of prey species, which, thus, rely upon flawless and working biological systems. Human exercises, like deforestation, territory discontinuity, and unlawful poaching, straightforwardly influence the feasibility of Sumatran tiger populaces.

Checking the situation with Sumatran tigers gives moderates and specialists significant bits of knowledge into the condition of the rainforest environment. Changes in tiger conduct, regenerative achievement, or populace thickness can be demonstrative of more extensive biological patterns. By understanding the difficulties looked by Sumatran tigers, moderates gain a more profound comprehension of the intricate connections inside the environment and can carry out designated techniques for its conservation.

Cornerstone Species in real life

Sumatran tigers, as cornerstone species, assume a crucial part in molding the construction and capability of their environments. The idea of cornerstone species, presented by biologist Robert T. Paine, stresses the unbalanced effect specific species have on their current circumstance comparative with their overflow.

On account of Sumatran tigers, their job as cornerstone species is clear in the guideline of prey populaces and the flowing consequences for vegetation and other fauna. The expulsion of tigers from the biological system could set off a trophic outpouring, prompting overgrazing by herbivores, exhaustion of plant assets, and resulting influences on more modest well evolved creatures, birds, and even bugs.

The impact of Sumatran tigers stretches out past direct predation. The apprehension imparted in prey species by the presence of these dominant hunters can make what is known as the "scene of dread." This mental scene shapes the way of behaving of herbivores, influencing their development examples and rummaging procedures. Thusly, the very scene itself changes because of the apparent gamble presented by tigers, bringing about a dynamic and consistently changing mosaic of territories.

Ecotourism and Monetary Importance

The magnetic charm of Sumatran tigers reaches out to their environmental importance as well as adds to their monetary significance through ecotourism. The presence of these tricky animals draws natural life fans and sightseers from around the globe, giving financial motivators to the preservation of their living spaces.

Ecotourism revolved around Sumatran tigers can add to neighborhood economies by making position, supporting nearby organizations, and producing income for preservation drives. Mindful the travel industry rehearses that focus on the prosperity of tigers and their environments can cultivate a manageable concurrence between financial turn of events and natural life preservation.

Additionally, the social and stylish worth of Sumatran tigers adds an immaterial aspect to their importance. These dominant hunters, with their glorious presence and emblematic reverberation, become representatives for the protection of biodiversity. Their reality improves the social legacy of nearby networks and adds to a worldwide appreciation for the natural worth of wild spaces.

The Hazards and Insurances

Notwithstanding their biological significance, Sumatran tigers face a variety of dangers that endanger their reality and, likewise, the strength of the environments they possess. Boss among these dangers is territory misfortune, driven by deforestation for rural extension, logging, and framework improvement. The contracting of their normal living spaces pieces populaces, reduces prey accessibility, and builds the gamble of human-untamed life clashes.

Unlawful poaching for the untamed life exchange represents a critical danger to Sumatran tigers. The interest for their body parts, bones, and skins powers an illegal market, driving these great animals to the edge of elimination. Preservation endeavors are additionally convoluted by the mind boggling organization of criminal associations engaged with the unlawful natural life exchange.

Environmental change adds one more layer of intricacy to the difficulties looked by Sumatran tigers. Modified atmospheric conditions, changing precipitation systems, and increasing temperatures influence prey accessibility and territory appropriateness. These climatic movements, combined with existing dangers, make an overwhelming situation for the drawn out endurance of these dominant hunters.

In light of these risks, a huge number of preservation endeavors and securities have been carried out. The foundation of safeguarded regions and natural life holds gives urgent asylums where Sumatran tigers can flourish undisturbed. Protection associations team up with administrative bodies, neighborhood networks, and worldwide accomplices to address the main drivers of tiger decline and carry out systems for natural surroundings conservation and reclamation.

Innovation assumes an imperative part in protection endeavors, with developments, for example, camera traps, satellite checking, and hereditary examination supporting scientists in understanding tiger conduct, development designs, and hereditary variety. Local area based protection drives connect with nearby populaces in the guardianship of their normal legacy, perceiving the harmonious connection between human prosperity and tiger preservation.

Future Pathways

As we examine the eventual fate of Sumatran tigers and their job in the biological system, it is fundamental to consider the more extensive setting of worldwide protection challenges. The protection of these dominant hunters requires an all encompassing methodology that resolves the interconnected issues of living space conservation, environmental change moderation, and the more extensive ramifications of biodiversity misfortune.

The economical concurrence of Sumatran tigers and human networks requires creative arrangements that balance the necessities of both. Local area commitment, feasible jobs, and training drives can encourage a common feeling of obligation for the guardianship of the rainforest. Saddling the capability of ecotourism as a protection instrument requires cautious preparation and the executives to guarantee that monetary advantages line up with the drawn out safeguarding of tiger living spaces.

Global cooperation stays irreplaceable in the work to save Sumatran tigers. Shared liability, information trade, and the pooling of assets are indispensable parts of a worldwide system for the protection of these dominant hunters and the environments they occupy. By tending to the underlying drivers of tiger decline, for example, living space misfortune and the unlawful natural life exchange, the worldwide local area can add to the safeguarding of biodiversity on a worldwide scale.

In outlining the future pathways for Sumatran tigers, recognizing the intrinsic worth of these dominant hunters past their biological roles is essential. The social importance, financial commitments through ecotourism, and the tasteful worth they bring to the world highlight the significance of protecting these great animals.

A Source of inspiration

In the fabulous embroidery of Sumatra's rainforests, the meaning of Sumatran tigers arises as a string that winds around together the mind boggling intricacies of life. As dominant hunters, watchmen of biodiversity, and marks of environment wellbeing, they exemplify the fragile equilibrium that supports the snare of life in these rich scenes.

The hazards looked by Sumatran tigers reverberation the more extensive difficulties going up against worldwide biodiversity and the honesty of normal frameworks. Their destiny is laced with the decisions mankind makes in the domains of preservation, reasonable turn of events, and environment activity. The source of inspiration resonates for the safeguarding of Sumatran tigers as well as for the protection of the very environments that support life on The planet.

The protection of Sumatran tigers requires an aggregate responsibility — from nearby networks to global partners — to address the multi-layered difficulties that undermine their reality. It requires a change in perspective in the manner we see and communicate with our normal world, perceiving that the prosperity of mankind is unpredictably connected to the soundness of the environments we share with different species.

As we set out on this excursion of protection, we should notice the illustrations murmured by the stirring leaves of Sumatra's rainforests and the quiet footfalls of its gatekeepers. The meaning of Sumatran tigers rises above the limits of science and nature; it incorporates the actual pith of our interconnected presence on this planet. In our decisions today, we shape the fate of Sumatran tigers and, in doing as such, graph a course for a more amicable and maintainable future for every single living being.

2. **Introduction to the unique characteristics and challenges faced by Sumatran tigers.**

In the core of the Indonesian archipelago, in the midst of the verdant scenes of Sumatra, lurks a grand and fundamentally jeopardized species: the Sumatran tiger (Panthera tigris sumatrae).

As a particular subspecies of the tiger family, the Sumatran tiger shows a bunch of exceptional qualities that recognize it among its catlike partners as well as inside the more extensive domain of biodiversity. This investigation digs into the particular characteristics that characterize Sumatran tigers and looks at the considerable difficulties they defy, from natural surroundings misfortune and poaching to the complexities of preservation even with an influencing world.

Particular Elements of Sumatran Tigers

1. **Morphological Wonders:**
Sumatran tigers, known for their minimal size and particular actual elements,

grandstand variations that mirror the island's remarkable natural setting. More modest in height contrasted with other tiger subspecies, grown-up Sumatran tigers normally weigh between 165 to 308 pounds, with guys being bigger than females. Their more little size takes into account upgraded dexterity, urgent for exploring the thick and complex landscape of Sumatra's rainforests.

Separating these tigers further is their rich coat, which sports a hazier orange shade and more unmistakable dark stripes contrasted with other tiger species. The dull, weighty stripes act as a striking difference against their lively coat, making a cover that helps them in the dappled daylight separating through the rainforest shelter. Furthermore, Sumatran tigers frequently gloat a thicker coat, a transformation to the cooler and wetter climate of their island home.

2. **Island Segregation:**

The uniqueness of Sumatran tigers isn't simply bound to their actual attributes however reaches out to their confined island presence. Cut off from central area Asia by rising ocean levels toward the finish of the last Ice Age, these tigers have advanced in detachment for millennia. This separation has prompted a particular hereditary cosmetics, stamping them as a hereditarily extraordinary and geologically disengaged populace.

Island environments frequently encourage remarkable transformations among species because of restricted assets and an absence of interbreeding with central area populaces. The transformative excursion of Sumatran tigers, molded by the difficulties and amazing open doors introduced by their island territory, adds to their particular hereditary character inside the more extensive tiger family.

Social Characteristics

1. **Single Stalkers:**
   Sumatran tigers, similar to their tiger family members, are single trackers, exploring the thick rainforest in a journey for prey. This single way of behaving isn't only a result of natural surroundings limitations yet a developed procedure for endurance in a climate rich with prey variety.

   The rainforests of Sumatra present a mosaic of natural surroundings, from thick vegetation to open clearings. The single idea of Sumatran tigers permits them to adjust their hunting systems in light of the fluctuated scenes they cross. It likewise limits contest for assets, guaranteeing a more proficient double-dealing of the prey an accessible in their area.

2. **Variation to Assorted Prey:**

The exceptional environmental setting of Sumatra's rainforests has affected the dietary inclinations of Sumatran tigers. Not at all like their cousins in additional open scenes, Sumatran tigers have adjusted to a different scope of prey, including different types of deer, wild hog, and other more modest vertebrates. This flexibility is a demonstration of their strength notwithstanding the consistently changing elements of their current circumstance.

The capacity to switch between various prey species is an essential method for surviving, particularly in a biological system where the overflow and accessibility of prey can vary. It likewise features the adaptability and cleverness innate in the conduct collection of Sumatran tigers.

The Dangers Looked by Sumatran Tigers

1. **Territory Misfortune and Discontinuity:**

   Regardless of their amazing transformations, Sumatran tigers face an existential danger stemming fundamentally from human-instigated changes to their territory. The uncontrolled deforestation in Sumatra, driven by rural extension, logging, and foundation advancement, has prompted the misfortune and discontinuity of their once-immense rainforest areas.

   As tractors and trimming tools infringe upon their hereditary domains, Sumatran tigers wind up progressively bound to separated patches of timberland. The fracture of their environment restricts their capacity to wander uninhibitedly as well as upsets basic biological cycles, for example, quality stream and the regular development examples of these lone hunters.

2. **Human-Untamed life Struggle:**

   The infringement of human settlements into tiger regions brings about an unpredictable snare of struggles. As urbanization and farming extend, the inescapable cross-over among human and tiger areas prompts elevated pressures. Tigers going after animals, retaliatory killings by disappointed ranchers, and the genuine danger to living souls make a perplexing scene of contention that risks the endurance of Sumatran tigers.

   The test of conjunction among people and Sumatran tigers is exacerbated by the lessening accessibility of prey in divided scenes. Tigers, driven by the need to make due, may wander nearer to human settlements looking for food, increasing the potential for struggle. Resolving this diverse issue requires preservation methodologies as well as maintainable job choices for nearby networks.

3. **Unlawful Poaching and the Natural life Exchange:**

The charm of Sumatran tigers reaches out past their natural significance to their stylish and financial worth. Tragically, this allure has made them an objective for unlawful poaching, driven by the interest for their bones, skins, and other body parts in the unlawful natural life exchange.

Poaching straightforwardly crushes tiger populaces as well as disturbs their social designs and hereditary variety. The deficiency of people, especially conceptive grown-ups, can have significant ramifications for the drawn out practicality of Sumatran tiger populaces.

Protection Difficulties and Systems

1. **Complex Preservation Scene:**
   Saving Sumatran tigers requires exploring an intricate scene of difficulties. The interconnected idea of issues, for example, living space misfortune, human-natural life struggle, and poaching requires comprehensive and interdisciplinary protection draws near.

   The viability of protection procedures depends on figuring out the perplexing snare of connections inside environments and tending to the main drivers of tiger decline. Traditionalists wrestle with the prompt dangers to tigers as well as with the more extensive issues of practical turn of events, land-use arranging, and human prosperity.

2. **Safeguarded Regions and Hall Creation:**
   Laying out and keeping up with safeguarded regions and untamed life halls address pivotal components of Sumatran tiger protection. Safeguarded regions give safe-havens where tigers can wander undisturbed, display normal ways of behaving, and add to the general soundness of biological systems. Untamed life passages, interfacing divided environments, work with the development of people between disengaged patches of woods, advancing hereditary variety and relieving the impacts of territory discontinuity.

   Compelling administration of safeguarded regions requires joint effort between legislative bodies, protection associations, and neighborhood networks. Guaranteeing the trustworthiness of these spaces includes tending to criminal operations inside and around these zones, implementing hostile to poaching measures, and dealing with the cooperations among tigers and close by human settlements.

3. **Local area Commitment and Supportable Vocations:**
   The outcome of Sumatran tiger protection relies on the dynamic association and backing of nearby networks. Drawing in with networks in the turn of events and execution of protection drives cultivates a feeling of shared liability and proprietorship.

   One key perspective is the advancement of manageable occupations that reduce strain on the rainforest and its occupants. Drives that give elective kinds of revenue, for example, local area based ecotourism, agroforestry, and reasonable horticulture rehearses, add to both neediness lightening and living space preservation.

4. **Innovation and Development:**

The preservation tool compartment for Sumatran tigers has extended with mechanical advancements. Camera traps, satellite checking, and hereditary examination assume significant parts in grasping tiger conduct, populace elements, and hereditary wellbeing. These devices help analysts and protectionists in get-together vital information, illuminating preservation systems, and observing the adequacy of mediations.

Development additionally stretches out to local area commitment, where versatile innovation and virtual entertainment stages are utilized for mindfulness crusades, detailing of untamed life sightings, and instruction drives. The utilization of innovation spans holes in correspondence, associates partners, and enhances the worldwide reach of preservation endeavors.

The Desperation of Protection Activity

As we peer into the complicated universe of Sumatran tigers, it becomes clear that the earnestness of protection activity isn't just an issue of saving a solitary animal groups yet shielding whole environments and the sensitive equilibrium of life they support. The difficulties looked by Sumatran tigers are significant of more extensive issues influencing worldwide biodiversity, environment trustworthiness, and the complicated connections among people and the regular world.

The source of inspiration resounds through the rainforests of Sumatra, provoking us to reconsider our relationship with the climate and the common obligation we bear for the protection of Earth's variety. The exceptional qualities of Sumatran tigers, sharpened through centuries of transformation, reverberation a significant message about flexibility, interconnectedness, and the natural worth of each and every species in the great embroidery of life.

A Common Obligation

All in all, the exceptional qualities and difficulties looked by Sumatran tigers epitomize a bigger story of preservation, manageability, and the many-sided dance among humankind and the normal world. Their unmistakable highlights, molded by the detachment of an island environment, and their social idiosyncrasies, sharpened through the never-ending battle for endurance, lay out a representation of strength and variation.

In any case, the difficulties they face - from territory misfortune and human-untamed life struggle to the always present danger of poaching - highlight the delicate idea of their reality. The direness of protection activity isn't simply a reaction to the predicament of a solitary animal types; it is an acknowledgment of our aggregate liability to shield the biodiversity that supports life on The planet.

As we explore the complicated territory of Sumatran tiger preservation, the way ahead requests cooperation, development, and a guarantee to address the main drivers of their decay. The destiny of Sumatran tigers is interwoven with our decisions, and the tale of their endurance is, eventually, a common story of trust, strength, and the persevering through potential for congruity among people and nature.

Chapter 1

The Enigmatic Sumatran Tiger

In the thick emerald domains of Sumatra's rainforests, a superb and mysterious animal holds influence - the Sumatran tiger (Panthera tigris sumatrae). As the littlest enduring tiger subspecies and one of the most basically jeopardized, the Sumatran tiger arises as an image of both the versatility and weakness intrinsic in the mind boggling embroidery of the normal world. In this far reaching investigation, we leave on an excursion into the core of the mystery that is the Sumatran tiger, unwinding its secrets, looking at the difficulties it faces, and imagining a future where the reverberations of its thunder keep on resounding through the rainforests.

The Captivating Persona of Sumatran Tigers

1. **The Dance of Shadows:**
   In the verdant profundities of Sumatra's rainforests, the subtle presence of Sumatran tigers summons a feeling of secret and wonderment. Dissimilar to their more prominent family members on the open fields, these tigers explore a world covered in shadows, moving with an elegance and covertness that adds to their confounding charm.

   The secretive idea of Sumatran tigers is profoundly implanted in their social variations. Singular and fundamentally nighttime, they wind through the underbrush, abandoning a path of mystery afterward. The stir of leaves, the flash of twilight on fur, and the frightful reverberation of a far off snarl - these pieces make the orchestra out of their reality, welcoming us to look into the shadows and ponder the secrets that exist in.

2. **Imagery in Culture and Legend:**

The perplexing air of Sumatran tigers stretches out past the domain of science to track down a spot in the social embroidery of the networks that share their living space. In neighborhood legends and old stories, these tigers frequently exemplify a duality - respected as gatekeepers of the woodland, yet dreaded for their likely risk.

The conjunction of adoration and dread mirrors the perplexing connection among people and the wild, adding layers to the confounding personality of these dominant hunters.

In Sumatran culture, the tiger frequently arises as an image of solidarity, power, and secret. It turns into a tribal portrayal of the untamed wild, an animal that strolls the line between the seen and the concealed. The reverberations of these social stories resound through time, winding around a story that mirrors the multifaceted dance among people and Sumatran tigers.

A More intensive Gander at Sumatran Tiger Science

1. **Unmistakable Actual Attributes:**
   Sumatran tigers stand separated because of their remarkable island beginning as well as with regards to their actual characteristics. Their moderately little size, dull orange coat, and intense dark stripes make a visual personality that recognizes them from other tiger subspecies.

   The development of these unmistakable highlights is a demonstration of the versatile excursion of Sumatran tigers in their island environment. Their conservative size upgrades nimbleness, working with development through the thick vegetation of Sumatra's rainforests. The hazier coat, with its extreme dark stripes, serves both as disguise in the dappled daylight and as a striking visual marker of their singularity.

2. **Hereditary Peculiarity:**

   Disengagement, the quiet planner of development, has shaped the hereditary character of Sumatran tigers into an exceptional work of art. Cut off from central area tiger populaces for millennia, they address an unmistakable hereditary genealogy. This detachment has added to their more modest size as well as made a permanent imprint on their by and large hereditary variety.

   The hereditary peculiarity of Sumatran tigers adds an extra layer to their puzzler. It highlights the delicacy of their reality, featuring the possible outcomes of losing even a solitary string in the many-sided embroidery of biodiversity. Understanding the hereditary subtleties of Sumatran tigers becomes fundamental with regards to preservation endeavors pointed toward protecting their special personality.

Gatekeepers of Biodiversity

1. **Dominant hunters and Environment Engineers:**
   Sumatran tigers rise to the peak of the pecking order, accepting the job of environment designers in the rainforests they possess. As top hunters, they organize the mind boggling dance of hunter and prey, molding the sythesis and elements of the whole biological system.

   The meaning of dominant hunters like Sumatran tigers reaches out past their nearby cooperations with prey. By controlling herbivore populaces, they forestall overgrazing and keep up with the equilibrium of plant networks. This, thus, encourages biodiversity, making a mosaic of living spaces that upholds a horde of animal varieties.

2. **Marker Types of Environment Wellbeing:**

In the complicated ensemble of the rainforest, Sumatran tigers arise as marker species, offering bits of knowledge into the general strength of their biological systems. Their prosperity is unpredictably connected to the accessibility and nature of their territory, making them sentinels that sign changes in the more extensive climate.

The decay of Sumatran tigers fills in as an unpropitious advance notice, a warning demonstrating disturbances in the sensitive harmony of their biological systems. Preservation endeavors zeroed in on saving these mysterious animals reach out past shielding a solitary animal groups; they become a guarantee to the comprehensive prosperity of whole environments.

The Shadows of Dangers

1. **Living space Misfortune and Fracture:**
   In spite of their tough nature, Sumatran tigers face imposing difficulties, the shadows of which pose a potential threat over their reality. Boss among these difficulties is territory misfortune, a steady juggernaut powered by human exercises. Deforestation, driven by agrarian extension, logging, and foundation advancement, cuts into the core of their rainforest homes.

   The outcomes of natural surroundings misfortune are significant. Sumatran tigers wind up bound to always contracting islands of green, secluded from one another and the more extensive environment. Discontinuity disturbs normal development designs, hereditary variety, and the fragile equilibrium that supports their reality. The shadows of tractors and trimming tools cast an inauspicious pall over the once-unassailable areas of these perplexing animals.

2. **Human-Natural life Struggle:**
   As human populaces infringe further into tiger domains, the shadows of contention strengthen. Sumatran tigers, driven by the instinctual need for endurance, may wander nearer to human settlements looking for food. Domesticated animals plunder and the genuine danger to living souls make a mind boggling trap of contention, further intensifying the difficulties looked by these perplexing watchmen of the rainforest.

   The shadows of contention address a fragile harmony between the requirements of neighborhood networks and the basic to protect the wild. Preservation methodologies should explore this nuanced scene, looking for arrangements that safeguard both human jobs and the perplexing occupants of the shadows.

3. **Unlawful Poaching and the Dull Exchange:**

The charm of Sumatran tigers reaches out past their biological significance to the shadows of a more obscure domain - the unlawful natural life exchange. Driven by interest for their bones, skins, and other body parts, these cryptic animals become items in a surreptitious commercial center.

Poaching annihilates tiger populaces as well as creates shaded areas over their social designs and hereditary wellbeing. The shadows of criminal associations engaged with the unlawful natural life exchange make many-sided difficulties for protectionists, requesting a diverse way to deal with battle this deceptive danger.

Protection Techniques in the Beginning of Trust

1. **Safeguarded Regions as Safe-havens:**
   Even with approaching dangers, safeguarded regions stand as encouraging signs in the preservation excursion of Sumatran tigers. These safe-havens, painstakingly outlined and made due, offer a shelter where tigers can wander undisturbed, show regular ways of behaving, and add to the more extensive strength of environments.

   Laying out and extending safeguarded regions requires a cooperative exertion including legislative bodies, preservation associations, and nearby networks. Successfully dealing with these asylums includes against poaching measures as well as resolving more extensive issues of natural surroundings safeguarding, feasible asset the executives, and local area commitment.

2. **Hallway Creation and Network:**
   The shadows of living space discontinuity can be scattered by the formation of natural life hallways that associate separated patches of woodland. These environmental halls act as life savers, permitting tigers and different species to cross scenes, advancing hereditary variety and moderating the effects of seclusion.

   Passageway creation requests an essential methodology, taking into account the regular development examples of tigers and the more extensive natural setting. It additionally includes drawing in with nearby networks to guarantee the practical utilization of scenes that exist in these essential connective tissues.

3. **Local area Commitment and Reasonable Occupations:**
   In the beginning of trust, local area commitment arises as a foundation of effective protection procedures. Enabling neighborhood networks to become stewards of their regular legacy cultivates a common obligation regarding the confounding animals that possess the shadows.

   Economical business drives, for example, local area based ecotourism, agroforestry, and manageable horticulture rehearses, offer elective ways that ease strain on the rainforest. The shadows of contention can be changed into cooperative endeavors where people and tigers exist together as one.

4. **Tackling Innovation for Preservation:**

The beginning of trust is enlightened by the beams of innovation, offering creative apparatuses for moderates. Camera traps, satellite checking, and hereditary examination give important experiences into tiger conduct, populace elements, and hereditary wellbeing.

The utilization of innovation stretches out past exploration to local area commitment, where versatile applications and web-based entertainment stages become conductors for mindfulness, schooling, and detailing of untamed life sightings.

In the interconnected universe of protection, innovation turns into a scaffold that traverses holes and enhances the aggregate voice for the safeguarding of confounding species.

Worldwide Coordinated effort and the Embroidery of Trust

1. **The Worldwide Goal:**

   In the beginning of trust, the shadows that undermine Sumatran tigers request a reaction that rises above borders. The riddle of their reality turns into a revitalizing point for worldwide coordinated effort, a common basic that perceives the interconnectedness of worldwide biodiversity.

   Global organizations unite mastery, assets, and an aggregate obligation to tending to the underlying drivers of tiger decline. The shadows of living space misfortune, poaching, and human-untamed life struggle track down no comfort in political limits, requiring a bound together exertion that broadens the embroidery of trust across landmasses.

2. **Promotion and Public Mindfulness:**

In the beginning of trust, the shadows disperse under the illumination of support and public mindfulness. The perplexing charm of Sumatran tigers turns into a reference point that causes to notice the more extensive issues of living space preservation, feasible turn of events, and the moral treatment of untamed life.

Support endeavors arrive at past the domains of protectionists, connecting with general society, policymakers, and powerhouses. The force of narrating, combined with the visual quality of these perplexing animals, makes a story that resounds with hearts and psyches, cultivating a worldwide local area joined chasing a common protection vision.

What's in store Spreads out

In pondering the fate of Sumatran tigers, the riddle that encompasses their reality turns into a powerful embroidery where strings of trust, difficulties, and aggregate activity are entwined. The shadows of dangers might persevere, however they are met with the beginning of trust - an expectation that imagines a reality where Sumatran tigers keep on meandering the rainforests, their mysterious presence reverberating through the ages.

What's in store spreads out with potential outcomes, dependent upon the decisions mankind makes today. The shadows might wait, however they are not inconceivable. Preservation endeavors, local area commitment, mechanical developments, and worldwide cooperation meet to make a story of versatility, variation, and concurrence.

In this unfurling future, Sumatran tigers arise as cryptic gatekeepers of the rainforest as well as envoys for a more extensive message - a message that addresses the characteristic worth of each and every species, the interconnectedness of life, and the common obligation we bear for the prosperity of our planet.

The Embroidered artwork of Concurrence

The mystery of Sumatran tigers allures us to disentangle the intricacies of their reality and, in doing as such, go up against our own part in the complex snare of life. As gatekeepers of biodiversity, sentinels of environment wellbeing, and images of social importance, Sumatran tigers encapsulate an embroidery of concurrence that stretches out past the limits of species and countries.

In the embroidered artwork of conjunction, the decisions today reverberate through time. The riddle of Sumatran tigers turns into a mirror mirroring our ability for sympathy, stewardship, and an agreeable relationship with nature. The shadows that undermine their reality are shadows projected by mankind, and the beginning of trust is a common dawn that enlightens a way toward a future where confounding animals meander indiscriminately, and the rainforests reverberation with the immortal ensemble of life.

1.1 Detailed exploration of the physical and behavioral characteristics of Sumatran tigers.

In the lavish rainforests of Sumatra, where emerald shelters embrace a rich embroidery of biodiversity, a stunning hunter sneaks - the Sumatran tiger (Panthera tigris sumatrae). This subspecies, interestingly adjusted to the island's landscape and environmental complexities, brags a collection physical and social qualities that recognize it inside the more extensive cat family. In this itemized investigation, we dive into the tastefulness and multifaceted design of Sumatran tigers, disentangling the subtleties of their actual traits and ways of behaving that characterize their baffling presence.

The Morphological Wonders

1. **Size and Height:**

   Sumatran tigers, prestigious for their minor size among their tiger family members, exemplify the rule of island dwarfism. Grown-up guys regularly weigh between 220 to 310 pounds, while females are prominently more modest, gauging around 165 to 243 pounds. This reduced height, a reaction to the requirements of island living, awards them improved spryness in exploring the thick vegetation of Sumatra's rainforests.

   The more modest size of Sumatran tigers is an immediate transformation to their island living space, where restricted assets and thick vegetation request a more lithe and flexibility hunter.

This size distinction likewise mirrors an articulated sexual dimorphism, with guys being fundamentally bigger than females, a trademark that impacts their social elements and regenerative ways of behaving.

2. **Coat Hue and Markings:**

The layer of Sumatran tigers is a work of art of regular imaginativeness, set apart by a rich orange tint that extends to a rosy tone. The dim, intense stripes that embellish their jacket make a striking visual difference, filling both stylish and useful needs. The force of the dark stripes, ostensibly more articulated than in other tiger subspecies, frames a particular example extraordinary to Sumatran tigers.

The complicated coat shading and markings of Sumatran tigers assume a diverse part. In the dappled daylight of their rainforest environment, the dim stripes give disguise, supporting their covert methodology during chases. Also, the one of a kind stripe design fills in as a singular identifier, working with acknowledgment among people and adding to their peculiarity inside the more extensive tiger family.

3. **Strong Form and Actual Variations:**

Sumatran tigers, in spite of their more modest size, display a powerful develop that highlights their fortitude and ability. Their appendages are strong and very much built, adding to their readiness and capacity to explore the fluctuated landscapes of Sumatra's rainforests. The forelimbs, furnished with sharp retractable paws, are considerable instruments for getting a handle on prey and climbing.

Quite, Sumatran tigers have variations custom fitted to their island climate. Their more strong bodies and more extensive skulls, contrasted with their central area partners, mirror the developmental reactions to the difficulties presented by the thick vegetation and various prey species tracked down on Sumatra. These actual variations line up with their job as dominant hunters in the many-sided snare of rainforest life.

The Dance of Shadows - Social Idiosyncrasies

1. **Lone Stalkers:**

Sumatran tigers, consistent with their lone nature, explore the shadows of the rainforest alone. Not at all like some other large feline species that display more friendly ways of behaving, these tigers are fundamentally singular trackers and drifters. The decision of isolation isn't simply a social characteristic yet a method for surviving sharpened over centuries.

The single idea of Sumatran tigers limits rivalry for assets inside their domains. It additionally lines up with the intricacies of their rainforest climate, where the thick vegetation and wealth of prey species make solo hunting more viable. This social idiosyncrasy guarantees a more proficient double-dealing of the different prey an accessible in their area, adding to their job as dominant hunters.

2. **Nighttime Travelers:**
The shadows of Sumatra's rainforests wake up as the sun sets, and the nighttime ability of Sumatran tigers becomes the overwhelming focus. These huge felines are principally crepuscular and nighttime, showing uplifted action during the front of obscurity. The shroud of night offers them an upper hand in both hunting and staying away from likely dangers.

The nighttime inclinations of Sumatran tigers line up with the way of behaving of their prey, which likewise will in general be more dynamic during the cooler evening hours. The dance of shadows turns into an ensemble of endurance, where the slippery developments of these tigers merge consistently with the beat of the rainforest night.

3. **Flexibility in Prey Choice:**

Sumatran tigers, consistent with their puzzling nature, exhibit a noteworthy flexibility in their decision of prey. Not at all like some tiger subspecies that might have practical experience in hunting explicit species, Sumatran tigers show a more pioneering approach, going after a different scope of animal types.

The versatility in prey choice is a reaction to the changed and dynamic environments of Sumatra's rainforests. From sambar deer and wild pig to more modest vertebrates and birds, Sumatran tigers exhibit an adaptability that guarantees their endurance in a climate where prey accessibility can be erratic. This social characteristic highlights their versatility and capacity to explore the intricacies of their island home.

Watchmen of Biodiversity - Biological Importance

1. **Dominant hunters and Populace Controllers:**
Sumatran tigers climb to the summit of the natural pecking order in the rainforests they possess, expecting the job of populace controllers. As dominant hunters, they assume an essential part in keeping up with the sensitive equilibrium of the biological system by controlling the wealth of herbivores.

The biological meaning of Sumatran tigers lies in their capacity to control prey populaces, forestalling overgrazing and keeping up with the variety of plant networks. Their presence guarantees the strength of the whole biological system, making a mosaic of territories that upholds a horde of animal categories. In this job, they arise as watchmen of biodiversity, forming the construction and elements of the rainforest.

2. **Pointer Types of Environment Wellbeing:**

The puzzling presence of Sumatran tigers stretches out past their nearby biological effect on a more nuanced job as pointer species. Their prosperity fills in as a gauge for the general soundness of their biological systems, mirroring the situation with environment quality, prey accessibility, and the effect of human exercises.

As sentinel species, Sumatran tigers pass on basic data about the condition of their current circumstance. Their decay or vanishing can flag disturbances in the fragile equilibrium of the rainforest, making traditionalists aware of hidden issues like natural surroundings misfortune, poaching, and human-untamed life struggle. In this limit, they become envoys for more extensive preservation concerns.

The Shadows of Dangers - Difficulties Looked by Sumatran Tigers

1. **Environment Misfortune and Fracture:**

   In spite of their variations and conduct characteristics, Sumatran tigers face imposing difficulties that cast shadows over their reality. First among these difficulties is the constant attack of living space misfortune and discontinuity. Human exercises, driven by rural extension, logging, and framework advancement, have cut into the core of their rainforest spaces.

   The outcomes of living space misfortune are significant. Sumatran tigers wind up restricted to separated patches of timberland, with normal development designs disturbed. Fracture hampers quality stream, limits admittance to prey, and decreases the general wellbeing of their populaces. The shadows of tractors and trimming tools compromise the domains of these mysterious hunters as well as the actual texture of their reality.

2. **Human-Natural life Struggle:**

   The shadows of human-natural life struggle pose a potential threat over the regions of Sumatran tigers. As human populaces extend and infringe into tiger natural surroundings, the inescapable cross-over brings about pressures. Tigers, driven by the instinctual need for endurance, may wander nearer to human settlements looking for food, prompting clashes with nearby networks.

   The shadows of contention manifest in different structures - from domesticated animals plunder to retaliatory killings by baffled ranchers. The danger to living souls makes a complex and nuanced scene where preservation endeavors should explore the sensitive harmony between safeguarding tiger populaces and tending to the real worries of nearby networks. The shadows of contention request arrangements that orchestrate the requirements of the two people and tigers.

3. **Unlawful Poaching and the Dull Exchange:**

   The charm of Sumatran tigers reaches out past the shadows of their rainforest regions to the furtive universe of unlawful poaching and the untamed life exchange. Driven by interest for their bones, skins, and other body parts, these baffling animals become survivors of a dim and illegal market.

   Poaching devastates tiger populaces as well as upsets their social designs and hereditary variety. The shadows of criminal associations engaged with the unlawful untamed life exchange make complex difficulties for progressives. The battle against poaching requests powerful policing well as cooperative endeavors to address the main drivers, including the interest for tiger items.

Protection Procedures - Enlightening the Way ahead

1. **Safeguarded Regions as Fortifications:**

   Even with approaching dangers, the foundation and viable administration of safeguarded regions arise as encouraging signs for Sumatran tigers. These safe-havens, painstakingly assigned to incorporate center tiger natural surroundings, act as fortresses where these mysterious animals can flourish.

   Safeguarded regions assume a critical part in protecting the uprightness of Sumatran tiger populaces. Viable administration includes hostile to poaching measures, territory reclamation, and checking of tiger populaces. Cooperative endeavors between legislative bodies, preservation associations, and nearby networks are fundamental to guarantee the supported progress of these asylums.

2. **Hall Creation and Network:**

   The shadows of natural surroundings discontinuity can be dissipated by essential passageway creation that interfaces separated patches of woods. These natural hallways work with the development of Sumatran tigers between divided environments, advancing hereditary variety and keeping up with populace availability.

   Passageway creation requests a thorough comprehension of tiger conduct and scene nature. Drawing in with nearby networks is essential to guarantee the progress of these connective pathways. The shadows of confinement can in this way be changed into interconnected scenes that permit Sumatran tigers to wander openly and keep up with solid populaces.

3. **Local area Commitment and Economical Occupations:**

   The beginning of expectation for Sumatran tigers depends on dynamic commitment with nearby networks. Engaging these networks to become stewards of their normal legacy cultivates a feeling of shared liability regarding the prosperity of these confounding hunters.

   Economical occupation drives assume a significant part in tending to the shadows of contention and environment debasement. Local area based ecotourism, agroforestry, and supportable rural practices give elective kinds of revenue that mitigate strain on the rainforest. The change of shadows into cooperative endeavors guarantees that the two people and tigers exist together as one.

4. **Mechanical Developments:**

The enlightenment of trust reaches out to the domain of innovation, offering imaginative instruments for the preservation of Sumatran tigers. Camera traps, satellite checking, and hereditary examination give significant information to grasping tiger conduct, populace elements, and hereditary wellbeing.

The utilization of innovation stretches out past examination to local area commitment. Portable applications and virtual entertainment stages become spans that interface moderates, nearby networks, and a worldwide crowd. The shadows of obliviousness and correspondence holes are dissipated by the radiance of mechanical development.

Future Pathways - Exploring the Shadows

1. **Worldwide Joint effort:**

   The shadows that compromise Sumatran tigers rise above the limits of countries. The puzzle of their reality requests a reaction that is worldwide in scope - a cooperative exertion that perceives the interconnectedness of environments and the common obligation regarding their safeguarding.

   Worldwide cooperation becomes basic in tending to the shadows of living space misfortune, poaching, and human-untamed life struggle. Information trade, asset pooling, and composed endeavors intensify the effect of protection drives. The shadows that undermine Sumatran tigers are dispersed by an aggregate obligation to their conservation.

2. **Promotion and Training:**

The way ahead includes promotion that enlightens the shadows of obliviousness and disregard. Bringing issues to light about the situation of Sumatran tigers, their natural importance, and the difficulties they face turns into an impetus for change.

Training drives, both locally and worldwide, add to a more profound comprehension of the confounding idea of these tigers. The shadows of detachment are dispersed by the radiance of information, encouraging a feeling of sympathy and direness for their protection.

1.2 Discussion on the distinct features that set them apart from other tiger species.

The universe of enormous felines is a domain of remarkable variety, every species introducing a one of a kind embroidery of qualities and variations. Among these great animals, Panthera tigris, generally known as the Bengal tiger, arises as a particular and notable subspecies. This conversation digs into the complex angles that put the Bengal tiger aside from its kindred tiger species, investigating its geographic reach, actual qualities, social characteristics, environmental transformations, preservation status, and social importance.

1. **Geographic Reach and Territory:**

   The Bengal tiger's geographic reach is principally amassed in the Indian subcontinent, crossing across India, Bangladesh, Bhutan, and Nepal. This unmistakable dispersion separates it from other tiger species, each with its own exceptional reach. The shifted scenes inside this district, including thick mangrove backwoods, rambling prairies, and deciduous timberlands, add to the Bengal tiger's versatility and different qualities. This natural surroundings variety leads to a plenty of environmental variations that recognize Bengal tigers from their partners in various locales.

2. **Actual Attributes:**
The actual elements of Bengal tigers structure a striking mosaic that separates them in the complicated embroidery of the tiger family. Grown-up male Bengal tigers regularly weigh between 400 to 600 pounds, with females being marginally more modest, going from 220 to 350 pounds. The coat hue is a rich orange tone embellished with unmistakable dark stripes, while the underparts are white. This one of a kind tinge supports disguising inside the different scenes of their territory, a variation finely tuned to their particular climate. Relatively, other tiger subspecies, like the Siberian tiger (Panthera tigris altaica), display varieties in size, fur thickness, and tinge, mirroring the transformations expected for endurance in their separate environments.

3. **Stripe Example and Rosettes:**
While all tiger species share the trademark dark stripes, Bengal tigers show a particular stripe example and game plan of rosettes that add to their distinction. The stripes on a Bengal tiger are by and large more various and firmly separated than those of other tiger subspecies. The rosettes, enormous spots with a dim boundary, are complicatedly stuffed across their bodies, making an outwardly unmistakable and hypnotizing design. Specialists and natural life aficionados frequently use these unmistakable elements for individual ID, featuring the significance of understanding the subtleties in stripe designs for compelling protection and the board procedures.

4. **Skull Morphology and Cranial Qualities:**
The morphological highlights of the skull and noggin give extra bits of knowledge into what separates Bengal tigers from their family members. Unpretentious contrasts in skull shape, dentition, and other cranial qualities have been distinguished, adding to the subspecies' peculiarity. These variations are results of development, molded by the particular environmental specialties Bengal tigers possess inside the Indian subcontinent. A similar investigation of skull morphology among tiger subspecies reveals insight into the developmental directions that have chiseled the novel highlights of Bengal tigers.

5. **Social Qualities:**
Social qualities offer a window into the versatile techniques that tigers utilize to flourish in their separate surroundings. Bengal tigers, formed by the different environments they occupy, show a scope of ways of behaving adjusted to their particular environmental factors.

Known for their adaptability in hunting procedures, Bengal tigers utilize following, ambushing, and swimming methods. This flexibility is a reaction to the shifted prey species accessible in their natural surroundings, going from deer and wild hog to fish in oceanic conditions like the Sundarbans mangrove timberlands. This social variety separates Bengal tigers, stressing the unpredictable connection between their ways of behaving and the environments they possess.

6. **Preservation Status and Dangers:**
Understanding the preservation status and dangers looked by Bengal tigers is significant for valuing the difficulties in protecting this subspecies. The Worldwide Association for Preservation of Nature (IUCN) orders Bengal tigers as imperiled, flagging the earnestness of protection endeavors. The dangers envelop environment misfortune, poaching, and human-natural life struggle, with each component collaborating particularly inside the setting of the Indian subcontinent. Protection challenges looked by Bengal tigers might vary fundamentally from those of other tiger subspecies, requiring custom fitted methodologies that record for the particular financial, social, and natural elements affecting their territories.

7. **Human-Flesh eater Struggle:**
A characterizing component of Bengal tiger preservation is the complicated dance between these dominant hunters and the human populaces occupying the locales encompassing their living spaces. The thickly populated regions abutting Bengal tiger domains frequently bring about human-meat eater clashes. Dissimilar to tiger populaces in additional distant areas, Bengal tigers habitually experience human settlements, prompting expanded episodes of domesticated animals predation and, tragically, retaliatory killings by neighborhood networks. Relieving these struggles requires a nuanced comprehension of the financial elements, land-use examples, and concurrence procedures, separating Bengal tiger preservation from endeavors zeroed in on other tiger subspecies.

8. **Social Importance:**
The social meaning of Bengal tigers in the districts they possess adds a layer of intricacy to their preservation story. Worshipped and representing strength, power, and persona, Bengal tigers assume a crucial part in neighborhood customs, legends, and folklore. This profound social association highlights the requirement for preservation procedures that incorporate nearby information, convictions, and practices. Not at all like other tiger subspecies, the social meaning of Bengal tigers significantly impacts the discernments and mentalities of nearby networks, requiring preservation moves toward that are socially delicate and comprehensive.

9. **Biological Variations:**
Bengal tigers, molded by the assorted biological systems of the Indian subcontinent, show special environmental transformations. The Sundarbans, a huge

mangrove timberland meeting India and Bangladesh, presents an unmistakable climate where Bengal tigers have created variations for swimming and hunting in water. This oceanic ability is an outstanding element that separates Bengal tigers from their landlocked partners. Conversely, Siberian tigers, adjusted to the unforgiving taiga woods, feature different biological transformations, for example, a thicker fur garment to endure cold temperatures.

Understanding these subspecies-explicit transformations gives significant experiences into the developmental cycles forming their particular elements.

10. **Collaborations with Prey Species:**

The cooperations between Bengal tigers and their prey species add to the subspecies' particular qualities. The different scenes of the Indian subcontinent support an assortment of prey, impacting the hunting systems and dietary inclinations of Bengal tigers. Understanding these elements includes looking at the coevolutionary connections between Bengal tigers and their prey, a feature that might contrast fundamentally from the collaborations saw in the environments of other tiger subspecies. The job of Bengal tigers as dominant hunters inside their environments highlights their natural importance and separates them with regards to their effect on nearby biodiversity.

11. **Hereditary Changeability:**

Hereditary examinations uncover the complexities of the developmental history and connections among tiger subspecies. Bengal tigers, with their particular hereditary markers and varieties, show a degree of hereditary variety that recognizes them from other tiger populaces. The protection of hereditary fluctuation is significant for the drawn out endurance and flexibility of the subspecies. Protection endeavors for Bengal tigers ought to consider the upkeep of hereditary variety as a key part, featuring the subspecies-explicit hereditary characteristics that add to its peculiarity.

Chapter 2

The Rainforest Habitat

The rainforest living space, frequently hailed as the World's lungs, remains as a demonstration of the miracles of biodiversity and environmental intricacy. This huge and mind boggling biological system, portrayed by lavish vegetation, high precipitation, and a large number of living things, assumes a urgent part in worldwide environment guideline. This exhaustive investigation dives into the complex components of the rainforest territory, inspecting its underlying layers, unmatched biodiversity, environmental capabilities, the squeezing need for protection, and the horde dangers it faces.

1. **Definition and Kinds of Rainforests:**
1. **Tropical Rainforests:**
   The expression "rainforest" principally alludes to tropical rainforests, arranged close to the equator and getting predictable precipitation over time. These lavish biological systems flourish in areas like Focal and South America, Africa, Southeast Asia, and portions of the Pacific. The Amazon Rainforest, the Congo Rainforest, and the rainforests of Borneo and Sumatra embody the variety and meaning of tropical rainforests.
2. **Mild Rainforests:**

Past the tropical belt, mild rainforests prosper in cooler areas like the Pacific Northwest of North America, southern Chile, and pockets of New Zealand and Australia. While offering a few highlights to their tropical partners, calm rainforests have remarkable transformations to colder environments, giving a particular biological viewpoint.

II. Construction of the Rainforest Natural surroundings:

1. **Covering Layer:**
   The rainforest natural surroundings is defined into layers, each adding to the biological system's many-sided balance. The shelter layer, comprising of the highest tree crowns, frames a thick mosaic of leaves, branches, and plants. This

top level is washed in daylight and houses a different cluster of animal types, including primates and different avian occupants.

2. **Understory Layer:**

Underneath the shelter lies the understory, portrayed by decreased light levels. This layer is a shelter for animal categories adjusted to bring down light circumstances, including creatures of land and water, reptiles, and more modest vertebrates. The understory has a remarkable arrangement of verdure, adding to the general biodiversity of the rainforest.

3. **Woods Floor:**

The woods floor, shrouded in a thick layer of decaying natural matter, is a powerful domain of supplement cycling. Bugs, growths, and detritivores take part in the decay cycle, enhancing the dirt and encouraging new vegetation. This layer assumes a crucial part in supporting the wellbeing of the whole rainforest environment.

4. **New Layer:**

Over the shelter, the emanant layer comprises of transcending trees that surpass the general shade level. These monsters have particular species adjusted to life in the upper scopes of the rainforest. The new layer adds an additional aspect to the living space, giving exceptional biological specialties.

III. Biodiversity in the Rainforest:

1. **Greenery:**

Tree Variety:

Rainforests are famous for their excellent tree variety. The Amazon Rainforest alone is assessed to hold onto more than 16,000 different tree species. This wealth adds to the general intricacy and flexibility of the environment.

Epiphytes:

Epiphytic plants, including orchids, bromeliads, and greeneries, flourish in the overhang by connecting to branches and trunks. These plants draw supplements and water from the air, adding an ethereal quality to the rainforest's upward scenes.

Restorative Plants:

Rainforests are mother lodes of restorative plants, with native networks depending on the rich natural variety for conventional medication. The revelation of new drug compounds frequently follows its foundations to these biodiverse environments.

2. **Fauna:**

Well evolved creatures:

Rainforests house a stunning assortment of well evolved creatures, from notorious species like panthers and ungulates to different monkey species. Nighttime animals like ocelots explore the understory, adding to the unique embroidery of rainforest life.

Birds:

Avian variety in rainforests is unmatched, with energetic parrots, toucans, and birds of heaven enhancing the overhang. The songs of these birds make a hear-able ensemble that resounds through the rainforest.

Creatures of land and water and Reptiles:

Frogs, snakes, reptiles, and other herpetofauna track down their specialties in the assorted microhabitats of the rainforest. Their presence shows the biological strength of these biological systems, as creatures of land and water, specifically, are viewed as signs of natural prosperity.

Bugs:

The bug variety in rainforests is faltering, enveloping endless types of butterflies, scarabs, insects, and different arthropods. These bugs assume vital parts in fertilization, decay, and supplement cycling, adding to the general working of the environment.

IV. Natural Elements of the Rainforest:

1. **Carbon Sequestration:**

   Rainforests go about as crucial carbon sinks, retaining and putting away critical measures of carbon dioxide through the course of photosynthesis. The broad biomass of trees adds to controlling worldwide carbon levels, assuming a urgent part in relieving environmental change.

2. **Oxygen Creation:**

   Photosynthesis, prevalently happening in the leaves of rainforest plants, discharges oxygen into the climate. Rainforests, frequently named the "lungs of the Earth," are essential supporters of the development of a significant part of the world's oxygen.

3. **Hydrological Cycle:**

   The thick vegetation in rainforests impacts nearby and worldwide weather conditions. Happening, the arrival of water fume from plants, adds to the development of mists and precipitation. This complicated relationship impacts precipitation designs and the generally speaking hydrological cycle.

4. **Biotic Associations:**

The rainforest is a phase for complex environmental collaborations, including cooperative, mutualistic, and cutthroat connections among its different occupants. Coevolution and reliance among species add to the flexibility and security of the environment.

V. Significance of Rainforest Preservation:

1. **Biodiversity Areas of interest:**
   Rainforests are perceived as biodiversity areas of interest, holding onto uncommonly elevated degrees of species extravagance and endemism. The deficiency of rainforest territory represents an immediate danger to endless plant and creature species, fueling the worldwide biodiversity emergency.

2. **Native People groups:**
   Numerous native networks call the rainforest home, depending on its assets for their occupations, social practices, and conventional information. Protection endeavors should focus on the contribution of these networks, recognizing their job as indispensable stewards of the backwoods.

3. **Environment Guideline:**

Rainforests contribute altogether to environment guideline, and their protection is fundamental for moderating environmental change. The annihilation of rainforest environment disturbs carbon sequestration, fueling a dangerous atmospheric devation and influencing weather conditions.

VI. Dangers to the Rainforest Environment:

1. **Deforestation:**
   One of the main dangers to rainforests is deforestation, driven by agribusiness, logging, and foundation improvement. Enormous wraps of rainforest are cleared for dairy cattle farming, soy development, and palm oil manors, prompting territory misfortune and discontinuity.

2. **Environmental Change:**
   Environmental change represents a danger to rainforest biological systems, influencing temperature and precipitation designs. Modified climatic circumstances might influence the circulation of species, disturb environmental connections, and add to the rising recurrence and force of outrageous climate occasions.

3. **Unlawful Logging and Poaching:**
   Unregulated logging and poaching of natural life present quick dangers to rainforest environments. Intriguing and jeopardized species are especially powerless, and the unlawful untamed life exchange adds to populace declines and biological system awkward nature.

4. **Mining and Framework Improvement:**
   Extractive enterprises, including mining and huge scope foundation projects, can devastatingly affect rainforest biological systems. Territory obliteration, water contamination, and soil debasement result from these exercises, further risking the soundness of the environment.

5. **Fire:**

Uncontrolled out of control fires, frequently exacerbated by human exercises, can attack immense areas of rainforest. The results are twofold, as flames straightforwardly obliterate living space as well as delivery a lot of put away carbon into the air, adding to environmental change.

VII. Preservation Endeavors and Drives:

1. **Safeguarded Regions and Stores:**
   Laying out and keeping up with safeguarded regions and stores is a foundation of rainforest protection. These regions act as shelters for biodiversity, empowering species to flourish without the prompt danger of environment annihilation.

2. **Manageable Improvement Practices:**
   Carrying out reasonable advancement rehearses, for example, agroforestry and eco-accommodating the travel industry, advances the conjunction of human networks and rainforest biological systems. Offsetting monetary interests with protection objectives is critical for long haul manageability.

3. **Native Freedoms and Association:**
   Perceiving and regarding the freedoms of native networks is vital to rainforest preservation. These people group frequently have important customary information about supportable asset the executives, and their dynamic contribution improves the adequacy of protection endeavors.

4. **Worldwide Participation:**

Given the transboundary idea of numerous rainforests, worldwide participation is fundamental for successful preservation. Cooperative endeavors among nations, NGOs, and worldwide associations are pivotal for tending to worldwide difficulties, for example, environmental change and unlawful untamed life exchange.

2.1Overview of the Sumatran tiger's natural habitat: the rainforests of Sumatra.

The Sumatran tiger (Panthera tigris sumatrae) remains as an image of the rich biodiversity and natural meaning of the rainforests of Sumatra. As the littlest and most basically imperiled tiger subspecies, the Sumatran tiger is interestingly adjusted to its regular environment, which envelops the different and rich rainforests of the Indonesian island of Sumatra. This complete investigation digs into the complicated parts of the Sumatran tiger's normal safe house, offering a point by point outline of the rainforests of Sumatra, their biological highlights, the particular variations of the Sumatran tiger, protection challenges, and the vital significance of saving this one of a kind environment.

1. **Geographic Setting:**
1. **Area:**
   The island of Sumatra, arranged in Southeast Asia, is the 6th biggest island

around the world and the biggest completely inside Indonesia. Sumatra's geological area close to the equator adds to its heat and humidity, portrayed by high temperatures and predictable precipitation, making ideal circumstances for the development of broad rainforests.

2. **Biodiversity Area of interest:**

Sumatra is eminent as a biodiversity area of interest, holding onto a stunning assortment of plant and creature species, a significant number of which are endemic. The rainforests of Sumatra are essential for the Sundaland area of interest, a district known for its remarkable biodiversity and one of a kind natural qualities.

II. Rainforest Biological systems of Sumatra:

1. **Outline of Rainforests:**
   The rainforests of Sumatra are important for the bigger Indonesian archipelago's rainforest environment, which incorporates the islands of Borneo and Java. These rainforests are described by elevated degrees of precipitation, establishing a rich and complex climate with different layers, including covering, understory, and woods floor.

2. **Floristic Variety:**
   The rainforests of Sumatra brag striking floristic variety, with a heap of plant animal groups adding to the unpredictable embroidery of the environment. The different verdure incorporates transcending emanant trees, epiphytes, restorative plants, and different orchid and greenery species.

3. **Faunal Wealth:**

The fauna of Sumatra's rainforests is similarly great, highlighting a wide cluster of animal types. Elephants, rhinoceroses, orangutans, and different primate species occupy the timberlands close by a plenty of bird animal types, reptiles, creatures of land and water, and bugs. The rainforest gives a mosaic of microhabitats that help this rich biodiversity.

III. The Sumatran Tiger: A Cornerstone Animal varieties:

1. **Outline of the Sumatran Tiger:**
   The Sumatran tiger, Panthera tigris sumatrae, is the littlest tiger subspecies and is endemic to the island of Sumatra. Perceived for its unmistakable dull orange coat and thick dark stripes, the Sumatran tiger has advanced novel transformations because of the particular attributes of its rainforest environment.

2. **Variations to Rainforest Living:**

Size and Nimbleness:

The more modest size of the Sumatran tiger contrasted with other tiger subspecies is a variation to exploring the thick undergrowth of the rainforest. Their decreased size upgrades readiness, permitting them to move through the perplexing landscape easily.

Cover and Stripes:

The dim orange coat with strong dark stripes fills in as compelling cover in the dappled daylight of the rainforest. This extraordinary tinge helps with following and ambushing prey in the shifted and testing scene.

Exclusively Island-Staying Tiger:

As the main tiger subspecies exclusively occupying an island, the Sumatran tiger has adjusted to the particular environmental circumstances and restricted scope of Sumatra. This disconnection has prompted unmistakable hereditary qualities, accentuating the significance of protection endeavors to save this extraordinary genetic supply.

IV. Preservation Difficulties:

1. **Environment Misfortune and Discontinuity:**

   The rainforests of Sumatra face extreme dangers from environment misfortune and discontinuity, fundamentally because of logging, agribusiness extension, and foundation advancement. The transformation of woods into palm oil estates and other land utilizes has prompted the separation of tiger populaces, expanding the gamble of inbreeding and diminishing hereditary variety.

2. **Unlawful Logging and Poaching:**

   The rewarding exchange unlawful wood represents an immediate danger to the rainforest biological systems of Sumatra. Moreover, poaching of tigers for their skins, bones, and other body parts stays a tireless test, exacerbated by request in unlawful untamed life markets.

3. **Human-Untamed life Struggle:**

   As human populaces grow and infringe upon tiger territories, occasions of human-natural life struggle increment. Tigers might go after domesticated animals, prompting retaliatory killings by neighborhood networks. Tending to this contention is critical for both tiger protection and the prosperity of nearby networks.

4. **Environmental Change Effects:**

Environmental change represents a danger to the rainforests of Sumatra, influencing temperature and precipitation designs. Adjusted environment conditions might influence the dissemination of key prey species, possibly influencing the prey-hunter elements of the Sumatran tiger.

V. Preservation Drives:

1. **Safeguarded Regions and Stores:**
   Laying out and keeping up with safeguarded regions and stores is a major

procedure for saving the rainforests of Sumatra and the Sumatran tiger. These regions give a shelter to natural life, including tigers, and add to more extensive scene level preservation endeavors.

2. **Manageable Land Use Practices:**
   Advancing reasonable land use rehearses, like affirmed economical ranger service and agroforestry, assists offset human requirements with protection objectives. Approaches that coordinate financial advancement with natural assurance are significant for the drawn out soundness of the rainforest biological system.

3. **Against Poaching and Policing:**
   Fortifying enemy of poaching measures and upgrading policing are fundamental parts of protection drives. Cooperative endeavors including neighborhood networks, legislative organizations, and non-administrative associations (NGOs) add to the insurance of tigers and their territories.

4. **Local area Commitment and Instruction:**

Connecting with neighborhood networks in protection endeavors is vital for progress. Local area based preservation programs that give elective occupations, include neighborhood occupants in observing and assurance exercises, and bring issues to light about the significance of tiger protection add to the general progress of drives.

VI. Ecotourism and Monetary Motivating forces:

1. **Supportable The travel industry:**
   Creating and advancing reasonable ecotourism drives can give monetary impetuses to neighborhood networks to preserve the rainforest natural surroundings. All around oversaw the travel industry can produce pay, set out work open doors, and add to the protection of biodiversity.

2. **Carbon Credits and Installments for Environment Administrations:**

Investigating creative monetary models, for example, carbon credits and installments for environment administrations, can monetarily reward networks and landowners for protecting the rainforest. These drives perceive the fundamental job of flawless woodlands in sequestering carbon and keeping up with natural equilibrium.

2.2Discussion on the importance of these rainforests for the survival of the species.

Rainforests, with their verdant shades, humming biodiversity, and unpredictable biological systems, stand as the gatekeepers of life on The planet. These rich living spaces are something beyond stunning scenes; they are fundamental repositories of hereditary variety and assume a significant part in guaranteeing the endurance of endless species. This extensive conversation digs into the complex significance of rainforests, investigating the environmental complexities, the advantageous connections that characterize these biological systems, and the squeezing need for purposeful preservation endeavors to shield the sensitive equilibrium of life inside.

1. Focal point of Biodiversity:

Rainforests are frequently hailed as biodiversity areas of interest, and which is all well and good. These environments, covering a simple 6% of Earth's territory surface, house roughly 80% of the world's earthly biodiversity. The astonishing assortment of plant and creature species found inside rainforests adds to the worldwide hereditary pool.

Biodiversity, the extravagance of life in the entirety of its structures, is a foundation of biological wellbeing, and rainforests are at the very front of keeping up with this variety.

Hereditary Supply:

Rainforests, with their bunch species, act as hereditary supplies. The different hereditary cosmetics of populaces inside these environments is a consequence of centuries of variation to explicit specialties. This hereditary variety isn't simply a demonstration of the intricacy of life inside rainforests however a pivotal figure the versatility and flexibility of species even with ecological changes.

Specific Specialties and Transformations:

The assortment of microhabitats inside rainforests upholds species with specific necessities. From the transcending overhang to the concealed understory, each layer has an alternate local area of life forms adjusted to the particular states of their current circumstance. This specialization is a demonstration of the multifaceted natural dance that has unfurled north of millions of years, bringing about species particularly adjusted to their specialties.

2. Cornerstone Species and Trophic Fountains:

Rainforests are dynamic frameworks where the connections between species are finely adjusted. Cornerstone species, frequently dominant hunters, assume outsized parts in keeping up with this equilibrium. These species apply hierarchical control on the biological system, directing the populaces of different species. The presence of cornerstone species guarantees the wellbeing and usefulness of the whole biological system.

Hunter Prey Elements:

Hunters in rainforests, like enormous felines or flying predators, control the populaces of herbivores. This guideline forestalls overgrazing and guarantees the essentialness of plant networks. The unpredictable dance of hunter and prey is a demonstration of the coevolutionary connections that have molded rainforest biological systems.

Trophic Fountains:

The evacuation or decline of cornerstone species can set off trophic fountains — flowing impacts all through the food web. For instance, a decrease in the number of inhabitants in a top hunter might prompt an excess of herbivores, affecting vegetation and possibly changing the environment for different species. Protecting rainforests and their cornerstone species is fundamental for keeping up with the fragile equilibrium of these trophic cooperations.

3. Environment Specialization and Endemism:

Rainforests give a mosaic of specific environments, each taking care of the one of a kind necessities of various species. The multifaceted design of the woods, with its layers and specialties, upholds a large number of organic entities. Numerous species have advanced to be profoundly particular, depending on unambiguous circumstances inside the rainforest for their endurance.

Endemic Species:

Endemism, the peculiarity where species are tracked down only in a specific geographic region, is predominant in rainforests. These species are frequently particularly adjusted to nearby circumstances and may not make due external their particular living space. Safeguarding rainforests is inseparable from shielding these endemic species, forestalling their termination notwithstanding natural surroundings misfortune and environmental change.

Microhabitats and Specialty Dividing:

Microhabitats inside rainforests consider specialty parceling — an interaction where various animal varieties coincide by using different natural specialties. The different exhibit of specialties inside the woods empowers a huge number of animal types to flourish without direct contest for assets. Safeguarding these microhabitats is significant for supporting the unpredictable trap of life inside rainforests.

4. Restorative Potential and Logical Revelation:

Rainforests have been named the "world's drug store" attributable to the large number of plant species with restorative properties. Native people group, with their profound association with the land, have bridled the mending capability of these plants for ages. The significance of rainforests for species endurance stretches out past the environment; it ventures into the domain of human wellbeing and logical disclosure.

Drug Potential:

Numerous cutting edge drugs have their foundations in compounds got from rainforest plants. From hostile to disease specialists to pain relievers, the drug capability of rainforest greenery is immense and to a great extent undiscovered. The deficiency of rainforests implies losing expected remedies for infections as well as an abundance of information held by native networks.

Bioprospecting and Moral Contemplations:

Bioprospecting, the quest for novel mixtures in living creatures, has been a subject of discussion. The moral contemplations of getting to hereditary assets from rainforests, especially without fair remuneration to native networks, highlight the requirement for capable and maintainable practices in logical investigation.

5. Carbon Sequestration and Environment Guideline:

Rainforests are vital players in the worldwide carbon cycle, filling in as significant carbon sinks. Through photosynthesis, trees assimilate carbon dioxide and store carbon in their biomass. The sheer biomass of rainforests makes them successful in moderating the effects of environmental change by decreasing the convergence of ozone depleting substances in the air.

Environmental Change Relief:

The protection of rainforests is a vital procedure in relieving environmental change. Deforestation discharges put away carbon back into the environment, adding to the nursery impact.

Safeguarding rainforests is, consequently, about protecting biodiversity as well as about battling the more extensive effects of environmental change on a worldwide scale.

Environment Adjustment:

The impact of rainforests reaches out past their job as carbon sinks. They likewise assume a part in controlling local environments, influencing precipitation examples and climate frameworks. Changes in land use, like deforestation, can upset these environment designs, prompting unexpected ramifications for both neighborhood and worldwide environments.

****6. Water Cycle and Hydrological Importance:**

Rainforests are unpredictably connected to the water cycle, affecting precipitation designs and keeping up with hydrological balance. Happening, the cycle by which plants discharge water fume, adds to cloud development and precipitation. The thick vegetation of rainforests holds soil dampness, forestalling fast spillover and soil disintegration.

Watershed Assurance:

Rainforests go about as normal wipes, engrossing and delivering water slowly. This sluggish arrival of water keeps up with the respectability of watersheds and lessens the gamble of floods and avalanches. The conservation of rainforests is fundamental for protecting water assets, helping both neighborhood environments and downstream networks.

Influence on Waterway Frameworks:

Changes in land use, like deforestation, can adjust stream frameworks, prompting expanded sedimentation and changes in water quality. The preservation of rainforests is critical for keeping up with the strength of waterway environments and the administrations they give to encompassing networks.

****7. Monetary Worth and Reasonable Jobs:**

Rainforests contribute altogether to neighborhood and worldwide economies through the economical utilization of their assets. Lumber, non-wood backwoods items, and eco-the travel industry are vital parts of rainforest economies. Offsetting monetary exercises with protection rehearses is fundamental for guaranteeing the proceeded with accessibility of these assets.

Economical Asset The board:

Manageable gathering of wood and non-lumber timberland items guarantees that financial exercises don't exhaust the assets on which they depend. Affirmation programs, for example, those for feasible ranger service, assist with directing capable asset the board rehearses.

Eco-the travel industry Valuable open doors:

The biodiversity and normal magnificence of rainforests draw in vacationers from around the world. Eco-the travel industry gives financial open doors to nearby networks while encouraging an appreciation for the significance of preservation. Mindful the travel industry rehearses are fundamental to forestall adverse consequences on delicate environments.

****8. Social Legacy and Native Insight:**

For native networks living in or close to rainforests, these environments hold significant social importance. The woods are not simply scenes; they are vital to the personality, otherworldliness, and conventional acts of native people groups. Safeguarding rainforests involves regarding and safeguarding the social legacy of these networks.

Customary Information and Maintainable Practices:

Native people group have an abundance of customary information about maintainable asset the executives, plant-based medication, and biological elements. Teaming up with these networks isn't just a question of moral obligation yet in addition a realistic way to deal with protection. Incorporating conventional insight into preservation endeavors upgrades the viability and supportability of drives.

Social Disintegration and Misfortune:

The infringement of outer impacts and the deficiency of customary grounds undermine the social respectability of native networks. Protection endeavors should perceive and address these dangers to guarantee that the social legacy of these networks is saved close by the biological systems they occupy.

****9. Dangers to Rainforests and Criticalness of Preservation:**

The complicated equilibrium of rainforest environments faces a variety of dangers, setting the endurance of species in danger. Understanding these dangers is vital for planning compelling protection systems.

Deforestation and Natural surroundings Misfortune:

The most quick and inescapable danger to rainforests is deforestation. Driven by logging, horticulture, and framework improvement, huge wraps of rainforest are cleared yearly. The change of forested land into rural regions, especially for cash crops like palm oil, represents an impending danger to the different species that call these environments home.

Human-Untamed life Struggle:

As human populaces venture into rainforest regions, clashes among people and untamed life heighten. Retaliatory killings of hunters, loss of prey species, and dislodging of neighborhood networks are ramifications of territory misfortune, further featuring the earnestness of protection endeavors.

Unlawful Logging and Poaching:

The interest for lumber and natural life items drives unlawful logging and poaching exercises. Unregulated abuse of rainforest assets adds to populace declines, environment lopsided characteristics, and the deficiency of significant species. Reinforcing policing hostile to poaching measures is vital for tending to these dangers.

Environmental Change Effects:

Environmental change represents extra difficulties to rainforest biological systems. Climbing temperatures, changes in precipitation designs, and an expanded recurrence of outrageous climate occasions can upset the fragile equilibrium of these biological systems. Species adjusted to explicit natural circumstances might confront provokes in acclimating to fast climatic changes.

Chapter 3

Conservation Status And Threats

Biodiversity, the many-sided trap of life on The planet, faces uncommon provokes as human exercises keep on reshaping scenes and change environments. Understanding the preservation status and dangers to biodiversity is fundamental for planning compelling systems to protect the fragile harmony between environments and shield the endless species that call our planet home. This extensive examination digs into the protection status of different environments and investigates the multi-layered dangers that jeopardize biodiversity.

1. Worldwide Protection Status:

IUCN Red Rundown:

The Global Association for Protection of Nature (IUCN) Red Rundown fills in as a thorough gauge of the preservation status of species around the world. It groups species into classes going from Least Worry to Basically Imperiled in view of elements, for example, populace size, living space reach, and patterns in populace decline or development.

Elimination Hazard:

Numerous species across various scientific categorizations face a raised gamble of eradication. The assignment of "Jeopardized" or "Fundamentally Imperiled" signals a high probability of elimination in the wild, while species delegated "Helpless" face a significant gamble. Understanding these classes focuses on protection endeavors and distribute assets where they are generally earnestly required.

Biological system Appraisals:

Past individual species, moderates additionally evaluate the situation with whole environments. Biological system appraisals consider factors like living space fracture, debasement, and the general strength of natural cycles. These evaluations give bits of knowledge into the more extensive difficulties confronting biodiversity and assist with illuminating scene level protection methodologies.

2. Dangers to Biodiversity:

Natural surroundings Misfortune and Fracture:

Natural surroundings misfortune is one of the main dangers to biodiversity. Human exercises, including horticulture, urbanization, and foundation advancement, bring about the change of regular living spaces into developed land, urban areas, and streets.

The fracture of environments segregates populaces, disturbs movement courses, and decreases the general size of reasonable natural surroundings.

Environmental Change:

Environmental change represents an existential danger to biodiversity by adjusting temperature and precipitation designs, causing ocean level ascent, and expanding the recurrence of outrageous climate occasions. Species adjusted to explicit climatic circumstances might battle to make due in quickly evolving conditions, prompting shifts in conveyance and possible annihilations.

Contamination:

Contamination, in different structures, unfavorably influences biodiversity across earthly, freshwater, and marine environments. Air contamination, water contamination, and soil pollution can hurt plants, creatures, and microorganisms. Pesticides and composts in horticulture, modern poisons, and plastic waste in seas add to the debasement of environments and posture direct dangers to species.

Overexploitation and Poaching:

The impractical reap of regular assets, including overfishing, overhunting, and unlawful poaching, comes down on numerous species. Overexploitation drains populaces, disturbs biological equilibrium, and prompts decreases in biodiversity. Famous species like elephants, rhinos, and tigers face the danger of poaching for their body parts or skins.

Obtrusive Species:

The acquaintance of non-local species with new conditions can adversely affect nearby environments. Obtrusive species may outcompete local species for assets, present new illnesses, or change the actual attributes of living spaces. The spread of intrusive species is worked with by worldwide exchange and travel, compounding their effect on biodiversity.

Sickness:

Arising irresistible illnesses can significantly affect untamed life populaces. Illnesses sent between species, like zoonotic sicknesses, can prompt populace declines or even eliminations. Environmental change and territory debasement might impact the circulation of infection vectors, adding to the spread of sicknesses among natural life.

****3. Contextual analyses on Undermined Biological systems:**

Amazon Rainforest:

The Amazon Rainforest, frequently alluded to as the "lungs of the Earth," faces serious dangers from deforestation, agrarian extension, and environmental change. Inescapable logging, change to pastureland, and flames add to environment misfortune, risking the rich biodiversity that portrays this notable biological system. The deficiency of the Amazon Rainforest jeopardizes incalculable plant and creature species as well as disturbs worldwide environment designs.

Incredible Obstruction Reef:

The Incomparable Obstruction Reef, the world's biggest coral reef framework, faces dangers principally connected with environmental change. Climbing ocean temperatures and sea fermentation, driven by environmental change, lead to coral fading and upset the development of coral states. Contamination from farming spillover and beach front advancement further intensifies weight on the reef. Preservation endeavors are fundamental to moderate these dangers and guarantee the endurance of the different marine life that relies upon the reef.

African Savannas:

The African savannas, home to famous species like lions, elephants, and giraffes, experience living space misfortune because of farming and metropolitan extension. Human-natural life struggle strengthens as untamed life environments shrivel, prompting clashes between nearby networks and creatures. Protection methodologies in savanna biological systems frequently include endeavors to adjust the necessities of both natural life and human populaces.

****4. Preservation Examples of overcoming adversity:**

Panda Preservation in China:

The goliath panda, a symbolic types of China, confronted serious dangers because of living space misfortune and discontinuity. Preservation endeavors, including environment security, reforestation, and hostage reproducing programs, have added to the recuperation of panda populaces. The renaming of pandas from "Imperiled" to "Helpless" on the IUCN Red Rundown mirrors the progress of designated protection drives.

California Condor Recuperation Program:

The California condor, a basically imperiled bird animal varieties, confronted dangers from lead harming, territory misfortune, and DDT defilement.

The California Condor Recuperation Program, including hostage reproducing, living space security, and lead decrease endeavors, has prompted an unobtrusive expansion in the wild condor populace. While challenges continue, the program shows the potential for purposeful preservation activities to save species from the edge of elimination.

Galápagos Islands Protection:

The Galápagos Islands, an extraordinary archipelago known for its endemic species and commitments to transformative science, confronted dangers from intrusive species and overfishing. Preservation endeavors, including destruction programs for obtrusive species, supportable the travel industry practices, and marine safeguarded regions, have added to the conservation of the islands' particular biodiversity.

****5. Preservation Procedures and Arrangements:**

Safeguarded Regions and Preservation Stores:

Laying out and successfully overseeing safeguarded regions and preservation saves is a central procedure for protecting biodiversity. These regions give places of refuge to untamed life, support regular natural cycles, and act as fundamental shelters for species under danger. Nonetheless, it is pivotal to address the difficulties of guaranteeing powerful authorization, local area association, and network between safeguarded regions.

Reasonable Asset The executives:

Executing feasible practices in asset the board, like maintainable ranger service, fisheries, and farming, is fundamental for moderating the effects of overexploitation. Offsetting human requirements with environmental supportability is critical for keeping up with the strength of biological systems and forestalling the exhaustion of regular assets.

Worldwide Joint effort and Arrangements:

Biodiversity preservation frequently requires global cooperation because of the interconnected idea of biological systems. Arrangements like the Show on Natural Variety (CBD) plan to advance worldwide collaboration in shielding biodiversity. Global endeavors can resolve issues like unlawful untamed life exchange, environmental change alleviation, and the security of transboundary biological systems.

Local area Inclusion and Native Information:

Connecting with nearby networks in protection endeavors is central for the outcome of drives. Native information, frequently established in hundreds of years of conjunction with environments, can give important experiences into feasible asset the executives and biodiversity protection. Regarding the freedoms and information on native people groups is fundamental for moral and successful preservation rehearses.

Schooling and Mindfulness:

Raising public mindfulness about the significance of biodiversity and the dangers it faces is a critical part of protection. Training drives, public effort, and missions add to encouraging a feeling of natural obligation. Educated and connected with networks are bound to help preservation endeavors and backer for arrangements that safeguard biodiversity.

****6. Future Difficulties and Open doors:**

Fast Urbanization and Framework Advancement:

The rising worldwide populace and fast urbanization present difficulties to biodiversity preservation. Framework advancement, including streets, dams, and metropolitan development, frequently brings about natural surroundings discontinuity and misfortune. Adjusting the necessities of a developing human populace with preservation goals requires inventive preparation and supportable improvement rehearses.

Arising Advances for Preservation:

Propels in innovation, including remote detecting, satellite checking, and man-made brainpower, offer new devices for preservationists. These advances empower more exact observing of environments, early location of dangers, and information driven independent direction. Utilizing these instruments can upgrade the proficiency and adequacy of protection techniques.

Environmental Change Transformation:

Environmental change is a general test that requires versatile preservation techniques. Environments and species might have to move their reaches because of changing climatic circumstances. Preservation arranging should consider the versatility of environments and the versatile limit of species to guarantee their endurance despite environment related difficulties.

Incorporation of Protection into Improvement Objectives:

Accomplishing manageable improvement objectives and moderating biodiversity are interconnected goals. Incorporating protection into more extensive improvement plans, like the Unified Countries' Feasible Advancement Objectives (SDGs), can guarantee that financial and social advancement doesn't come to the detriment of biological systems and biodiversity.

3.1 Analysis of the current conservation status of Sumatran tigers.

The Sumatran tiger (Panthera tigris sumatrae) remains as a magnetic and imperiled subspecies, meaningful of the rich biodiversity tracked down on the Indonesian island of Sumatra. As one of the final territories for tigers, Sumatra faces various difficulties, going from natural surroundings misfortune to poaching and human-untamed life clashes. This investigation dives into the ongoing preservation status of Sumatran tigers, looking at the dangers they face, progressing protection endeavors, and the possibilities for guaranteeing the endurance of this fundamentally jeopardized subspecies.

****1. Conveyance and Environment of Sumatran Tigers:**

Extraordinary Environments of Sumatra:

Sumatra, the 6th biggest island internationally, flaunts interesting environments that help a different scope of widely varied vegetation. The island's tropical rainforests, peatlands, and montane environments give ideal natural surroundings to Sumatran tigers. The species is adjusted to various conditions, from swamp timberlands to sloping areas.

Contracting Territory:

In spite of the biological extravagance of Sumatra, the island has seen broad deforestation and living space misfortune throughout the long term. Logging, farming extension, and foundation advancement have brought about the discontinuity and debasement of tiger natural surroundings. Huge scope palm oil ranches, specifically, have been a critical driver of deforestation, further worsening the difficulties looked by Sumatran tigers.

****2. Populace Status and Decline:**

Current Populace Appraisals:

Assessing the specific populace of Sumatran tigers is trying because of the thick and distant nature of their environments. Nonetheless, current appraisals recommend that less than 400 people might stay in nature. This disturbing figure mirrors a huge decay from verifiable populace levels and features the critical requirement for preservation mediations.

Dangers to Populace Reasonability:

The decrease in Sumatran tiger populaces can be credited to a mix of variables. Territory misfortune, driven by deforestation and land change, is an essential danger. As the leftover environments become progressively divided, tigers face difficulties in tracking down mates, keeping up with hereditary variety, and getting to reasonable prey.

****3. Dangers to Sumatran Tigers:**

Natural surroundings Misfortune and Discontinuity:

The transformation of timberlands into horticultural land, especially for palm oil ranches, represents a serious danger to Sumatran tigers. Discontinuity of their territories disengages populaces, restricting quality stream and expanding the gamble of inbreeding. It additionally opens tigers to expanded human-natural life clashes as they adventure into adjusted scenes looking for prey.

Poaching and Unlawful Exchange:

Poaching stays a critical danger to Sumatran tigers, driven by interest for their body parts and bones in customary Asian medication. The unlawful natural life exchange, energized by worldwide business sectors, further fuels the gamble to these huge felines. Reinforcing against poaching endeavors and tending to interest for tiger items are critical parts of preservation methodologies.

Human-Natural life Clashes:

As human populaces grow and infringe upon tiger living spaces, clashes among people and tigers heighten. Tigers might go after animals, prompting retaliatory killings by nearby networks. Powerful techniques for relieving human-untamed life clashes include local area commitment, carrying out precaution gauges, and laying out safeguarded halls for tigers to move securely between divided environments.

Environmental Change Effects:

Environmental change represents extra difficulties to Sumatran tigers and their territories. Modified precipitation designs, climbing temperatures, and an expansion in outrageous climate occasions can upset the fragile natural equilibrium. Changes in prey accessibility and changes in vegetation cover might additionally pressure tiger populaces.

****4. Protection Endeavors:**

Safeguarded Regions and Protection Stores:

Laying out and really overseeing safeguarded regions is a foundation of Sumatran tiger protection. These regions, for example, public parks and untamed life holds, act as shelters where tigers can wander, chase, and breed without prompt dangers from human exercises. Reinforcing the implementation of safeguarded regions is urgent for defending tiger living spaces.

Against Poaching Measures:

Against poaching endeavors center around hindering and catching people engaged with the unlawful hunting of tigers. This incorporates expanding watches, using innovation, for example, camera traps, and drawing in neighborhood networks as watchmen of the tigers. Coordinated effort between policing, preservation associations, and nearby networks is fundamental for powerful enemy of poaching drives.

Natural surroundings Reclamation and Availability:

Restoring corrupted environments and reestablishing backwoods network are necessary parts of protection methodologies. Drives focused on reforestation and laying out natural life hallways work with the development of tigers between divided living spaces, upgrading hereditary variety and supporting long haul populace feasibility.

Local area Inclusion and Economical Turn of events:

Connecting with nearby networks in preservation endeavors is imperative for the outcome of drives. Maintainable improvement programs that offer elective occupations, advance eco-accommodating practices, and include neighborhood networks in navigation add to the concurrence of people and tigers. Building mindfulness and cultivating a feeling of stewardship among neighborhood occupants are key components of local area driven protection.

****5. Victories and Difficulties in Sumatran Tiger Protection:**

Tiger Preservation Scenes:

Tiger Preservation Scenes (TCLs) are enormous scope drives that plan to moderate tiger environments and advance scene level protection. In Sumatra, TCLs include composed endeavors between state run administrations, non-legislative associations (NGOs), and neighborhood networks. These scenes focus on the network of tiger environments, guaranteeing that tigers can move uninhibitedly across safeguarded regions.

Challenges in Requirement and Administration:

In spite of the headway made, challenges continue upholding preservation regulations and guaranteeing powerful administration. Powerless policing, and inadequate assets frustrate the execution of preservation measures. Tending to these difficulties requires coordinated effort between administrative bodies, NGOs, and global associations to reinforce lawful systems and upgrade implementation capacities.

Offsetting Protection with Advancement Needs:

Adjusting the preservation of Sumatran tigers with the formative necessities of neighborhood networks is a continuous test. Monetary tensions and the interest for land for farming and foundation advancement frequently struggle with protection objectives. Supportable improvement rehearses that incorporate preservation into land-use arranging are fundamental for tending to this test.

****6. Global Cooperation and Subsidizing:**

Worldwide Tiger Drive:

The Worldwide Tiger Drive, sent off by the World Bank and the Worldwide Climate Office, expects to twofold the quantity of wild tigers by 2022. This global exertion includes cooperation between tiger-range nations, NGOs, and the confidential area. While progress has been made in certain districts, the special difficulties looked by Sumatran tigers highlight the requirement for designated mediations.

Financing and Altruism:

Satisfactory financing is urgent for carrying out protection drives successfully. Magnanimous associations, legislative awards, and global assets assume an imperative part in supporting Sumatran tiger preservation. Guaranteeing supported subsidizing for long haul projects is fundamental for the outcome of endeavors to safeguard these jeopardized huge felines.

****7. Examination and Checking:**

Logical Exploration and Information Assortment:

Progressing logical exploration and information assortment are fundamental for figuring out the environment, conduct, and wellbeing of Sumatran tigers. Propels in innovation, including camera traps, satellite following, and hereditary examination, give important experiences into tiger populaces. Long haul observing permits traditionalists to evaluate the adequacy of mediations and adjust procedures in view of arising data.

Hereditary Variety and Wellbeing:

Keeping up with hereditary variety inside Sumatran tiger populaces is basic for their drawn out endurance. Inbreeding melancholy, coming about because of little and disengaged populaces, can prompt decreased wellness and expanded weakness to illnesses. Hereditary examinations assist with recognizing populaces in danger and illuminate movement endeavors to improve hereditary variety.

****8. Schooling and Promotion:**

Public Mindfulness Missions:

Schooling and public mindfulness crusades are instrumental in accumulating support for Sumatran tiger protection. These drives mean to educate people in general about the significance regarding tigers in keeping up with biological equilibrium and the dangers they face. Backing endeavors influence public opinion to impact strategy choices and advance manageable practices.

Schooling in Neighborhood People group:

Designated schooling programs in neighborhood networks add to encouraging a feeling of satisfaction and obligation regarding Sumatran tigers. Instructive drives frequently include school programs, local area studios, and the combination of preservation topics into nearby educational plans. Engaging nearby networks with information upgrades their job as stewards of the climate.

****9. The Job of Innovation in Preservation:**

Remote Detecting and GIS:

Remote detecting and Geographic Data Frameworks (GIS) assume a vital part in observing area use changes and surveying the effect of deforestation on tiger environments. Satellite symbolism gives continuous information that illuminates preservation techniques and distinguishes need regions for assurance and rebuilding.

Camera Traps and Checking Gadgets:

Camera traps have altered untamed life checking, permitting specialists to notice tiger conduct, gauge populace measures, and distinguish people. Furthermore, the utilization of collars furnished with GPS and other observing gadgets empowers constant following of tiger developments, giving important experiences to natural surroundings the board and against poaching endeavors.

****10. Future Possibilities and Proposals:**

Incorporated Scene Approaches:

Taking on incorporated scene moves toward that consider the requirements of the two tigers and nearby networks is urgent. These methodologies include economical land-use arranging, natural surroundings reclamation, and the formation of hallways that permit tigers to move openly between safeguarded regions. Cooperative endeavors among government organizations, NGOs, and networks are fundamental for the outcome of coordinated scene draws near.

Tending to Main drivers of Deforestation:

To guarantee the drawn out endurance of Sumatran tigers, it is crucial for address the underlying drivers of deforestation, including the development of palm oil manors. Economical farming practices, affirmation programs for capable land use, and buyer mindfulness missions can add to decreasing the interest for items connected to deforestation.

Local area Based Protection Models:

Enabling nearby networks as dynamic members in preservation is basic. Local area based protection models, where nearby occupants are straightforwardly engaged with direction and advantage from preservation endeavors, have demonstrated effective in different districts. These models adjust protection objectives to the prosperity of networks, encouraging a feeling of shared liability.

Worldwide Joint effort and Promotion:

Worldwide coordinated effort stays fundamental in tending to the worldwide idea of natural life protection. Support at global discussions, joint effort among NGOs and legislatures, and the sharing of best practices add to a planned and powerful methodology. Promotion endeavors can likewise assist with raising the profile of Sumatran tiger protection on the worldwide stage.

3.2Examination of the primary threats, including habitat loss, poaching, and human-wildlife conflict.

The protection of biodiversity is a worldwide objective, yet various species face critical dangers that risk their endurance. Among the essential dangers, territory misfortune, poaching, and human-untamed life struggle arise as key supporters of the decay of numerous species around the world. This assessment digs into the mind boggling elements of these dangers, investigating their underlying drivers, outcomes, and expected answers for cultivate a superior comprehension of the difficulties confronting natural life preservation.

****1. Territory Misfortune: A Quiet Threat:**

Deforestation and Land Transformation:

Territory misfortune, fundamentally determined by deforestation and land transformation, remains as one of the principal dangers to untamed life. Human exercises, like logging, agribusiness, and urbanization, bring about the getting free from tremendous regions of regular natural surroundings. This change wipes out basic biological systems as well as sections the leftover natural surroundings, separating populaces and blocking fundamental environmental cycles.

Influence on Biodiversity:

The outcomes of living space misfortune are significant, influencing biodiversity at different levels. Species dependent on unambiguous natural surroundings, from tropical rainforests to savannas, lose their homes and battle to track down appropriate substitutions. Living space discontinuity disturbs relocation courses, modifies hunter prey elements, and blocks the regular progression of hereditary variety inside populaces.

Danger to Expert Species:

Expert species, adjusted to specific conditions, face uplifted weakness. The deficiency of their particular living spaces leaves them with restricted choices for endurance. Animals like the Sumatran tiger, dependent on the thick rainforests of Sumatra, stand up to expanded dangers as their living spaces psychologist and piece, putting them near the very edge of eradication.

****2. Poaching: The Unrelenting Attack on Natural life:**

Driven by Request:

Poaching, the unlawful hunting or catching of wild creatures, stays an unavoidable danger powered by the interest for natural life items. Customary Asian medication, decorative things, and extraordinary pets are among the items driving poaching exercises. The interest for rhino horns, elephant ivory, and tiger bones represents the worthwhile business sectors that support this illegal exchange.

Influence on Jeopardized Species:

Jeopardized species, specifically, endure the worst part of poaching. Rhinos and elephants, focused on for their horns and tusks, face serious populace declines. The lofty tiger, worshipped in conventional medication, defies persevering mistreatment for its body parts. The deficiency of individual creatures upsets environments, debilitates hereditary variety, and hampers the general strength of species populaces.

Connections to Coordinated Wrongdoing:

Poaching frequently works inside the domain of coordinated wrongdoing, with deep rooted networks taking advantage of powerless policing permeable boundaries. The contribution of criminal organizations in untamed life dealing further confuses protection endeavors. Handling poaching requires natural life centered mediations as well as resolving the more extensive issue of coordinated wrongdoing.

**3. Human-Untamed life Struggle: The Guarantee Result of Concurrence:

Infringement and Territory Fracture:

As human populaces grow, they infringe upon untamed life living spaces, prompting uplifted occasions of human-natural life struggle. Territory fracture worsens this contention, driving creatures into more modest and more segregated regions where they come into direct contact with human settlements.

Crop Assaulting and Animals Predation:

In districts where farming is a predominant land use, natural life might strike yields or go after animals, prompting financial misfortunes for nearby networks. Elephants, for example, may pulverize crops, while hunters like lions or panthers can represent a danger to animals. Accordingly, ranchers might depend on retaliatory killings of untamed life, propagating a pattern of contention.

Wellbeing Worries for People:

Past financial effects, human-natural life struggle raises wellbeing worries for networks living in nearness to natural life. Assaults on people by huge hunters, like enormous felines or bears, bring out dread and outrage, frequently bringing about deadly measures against the creatures in question. Tending to these struggles requires adjusting the necessities of both natural life and human populaces.

**4. Protection Procedures and Moderation Measures:

Safeguarded Regions and Passageway Creation:

Laying out and really overseeing safeguarded regions is pivotal for protecting biodiversity. These regions act as shelters for untamed life, giving undisturbed natural surroundings where species can flourish. Furthermore, making untamed life halls interfacing divided environments works with the development of creatures and mitigates the effect of natural surroundings misfortune.

Manageable Land-Use Arranging:

Coordinating protection into land-use arranging is fundamental for accomplishing a harmony between human turn of events and natural life conservation. Economical horticulture rehearses, dependable logging, and metropolitan arranging that considers the necessities of untamed life add to limiting natural surroundings misfortune. Co-operative endeavors including state run administrations, NGOs, and neighborhood networks are imperative for fruitful execution.

Against Poaching Drives and Policing:

Reinforcing hostile to poaching drives and further developing policing basic parts of untamed life preservation. Preparing and preparing officers, utilizing present day reconnaissance advancements, for example, robots and camera traps, and encouraging worldwide cooperation improve the viability of hostile to poaching endeavors. Tending to the underlying drivers of poaching, including request decrease crusades, is similarly significant.

Local area Commitment and Training:

Connecting with nearby networks as dynamic members in preservation endeavors is basic. Local area based preservation models, where occupants are engaged with dynamic cycles and advantage straightforwardly from protection results, have demonstrated fruitful. Schooling programs that bring issues to light about the worth of natural life and encourage a feeling of stewardship add to long haul conjunction.

Natural life amicable Practices and Elective Vocations:

Advancing untamed life well disposed rehearses in agribusiness, for example, the utilization of obstacles to forestall crop attacks, decreases clashes among people and untamed life. Moreover, giving elective livelihoods, for example, eco-the travel industry or feasible asset the executives, offers monetary motivators for networks to effectively take part in preservation as opposed to depending on rehearses that hurt untamed life.

Lawful Systems and Worldwide Participation:

Upholding and upgrading lawful systems for untamed life insurance is fundamental. Nations should reinforce their regulation against poaching and unlawful natural life exchange, forcing tough punishments for guilty parties. Worldwide participation, worked with through arrangements and shows, upholds an organized reaction to transboundary protection challenges and the dealing of untamed life items.

****5. Examples of overcoming adversity and Progressing Difficulties:**

Progress in Tiger Protection:

Protection endeavors zeroed in on tiger populaces in specific areas have yielded positive outcomes. Drives in India, for instance, have added to an expansion in tiger numbers through territory security, hostile to poaching measures, and local area contribution. The bounce back of tiger populaces grandstands the potential for designated intercessions to have a huge effect.

Challenges in African Elephant Preservation:

African elephants, confronting persevering poaching for ivory, feature the continuous difficulties in protection. Regardless of global restrictions on ivory exchange, request endures, and criminal organizations keep on taking advantage of shortcomings in policing. Adjusting the preservation needs of elephants with the financial interests of neighborhood networks stays a mind boggling and progressing challenge.

Human-Natural life Struggle in Agribusiness ruled Scenes:

In scenes overwhelmed by farming, human-natural life struggle stays a relentless test. Crop attacking by elephants in pieces of Africa and Asia or predation on animals by huge carnivores requires setting explicit arrangements. Executing powerful measures that safeguard the two livelihoods and natural life in these mind boggling situations requires a nuanced and versatile methodology.

****6. The Job of Worldwide Drives and Public Promotion:**

Worldwide Preservation Drives:

Worldwide drives, like the Show on Organic Variety (CBD) and the Assembled Countries Economical Advancement Objectives (SDGs), highlight the significance of biodiversity protection. These stages give structures to worldwide coordinated effort and set focuses for the assurance of environments and species. The Aichi Biodiversity Targets, a piece of the CBD, explicitly address the decrease of territory misfortune and reasonable asset the board.

Public Support and Shopper Mindfulness:

Public backing assumes a vital part in forming preservation results. Mindfulness crusades, drove by ecological associations, researchers, and VIPs, illuminate the general population about the outcomes regarding living space misfortune, poaching, and human-untamed life struggle. Buyer mindfulness crusades focusing on the interest for untamed life items add to decreasing the market influences driving unlawful exchange.

Chapter 4

Guardians Of The Rainforest

The rainforest, frequently alluded to as the "lungs of the Earth," is a biodiverse and environmentally basic biological system that assumes a crucial part in worldwide environment guideline. In the midst of the rich coverings and energetic biodiversity, native networks arise as the gatekeepers of these priceless biological systems. This investigation dives into the imperative pretended by native people groups in rainforest preservation, looking at their conventional information, manageable practices, and the difficulties they face in the continuous battle to safeguard their hereditary terrains.

1. Social Association and Conventional Information:

Hundreds of years of Conjunction:

Native people group have occupied rainforest locales for a really long time, encouraging a profound and harmonious relationship with these biological systems. Their social characters are complicatedly connected to the land, as reflected in their profound convictions, customary practices, and public lifestyle. The rainforest, for the overwhelming majority native gatherings, isn't simply an asset to be taken advantage of however a consecrated space that maintains and feeds life.

Conventional Natural Information:

Native people groups have an abundance of conventional natural information went down through ages. This information envelops a cozy comprehension of the rainforest's greenery, fauna, and many-sided environmental cycles. From restorative plants to maintainable gathering rehearses, native networks have sharpened their mastery over hundreds of years, making a repository of shrewdness that adds to the protection of biodiversity.

Practical Asset The board:

Native asset the board rehearses are established in supportability and correspondence. As opposed to taking part in shifty or extractive exercises, numerous native gatherings training rotational cultivating, permitting environments to normally recover. Customary farming techniques, for example, agroforestry and swidden horticulture, show an agreeable harmony between human requirements and the conservation of biodiversity.

2. Safeguarding of Biodiversity:

Gatekeepers of Biodiversity:

Native people group go about as the caretakers of rainforest biodiversity, assuming a significant part in keeping up with the fragile equilibrium of biological systems. Their feasible practices add to the protection of assorted plant and creature species, guaranteeing the wellbeing and strength of the rainforest. Numerous species have coevolved with native networks, depending on their stewardship for endurance.

Assurance of Imperiled Species:

Jeopardized species frequently track down shelter in the regions of native people groups. The shortfall of enormous scope modern exercises here makes safe-havens where species like pumas, ungulates, and different primates can flourish. The interconnected snare of life in the rainforest depends on the presence of these cornerstone species, and native guardianship helps shield their natural surroundings.

Social Cornerstone Species:

A few animal groups hold social importance for native networks, filling in as social cornerstone species. These species are essential to the social character, otherworldliness, and conventional acts of native people groups. The security of these species isn't simply a biological basic however a social obligation regarding native networks.

3. Difficulties to Native Rainforest Guardianship:

Land Infringement and Deforestation:

Native terrains face consistent dangers from outer powers, including legislatures, agribusiness, and unlawful lumberjacks. Land infringement and deforestation imperil the domains that native networks rely upon for their jobs and social practices. As these outer tensions strengthen, native guardianship is progressively tested.

Absence of Legitimate Acknowledgment:

Numerous native networks need legitimate acknowledgment of their territory freedoms, leaving them powerless against double-dealing. State run administrations might allow concessions for logging, mining, or agribusiness on native regions without getting the free, earlier, and educated assent regarding the networks. This absence of legitimate insurance sabotages the capacity of native people groups to satisfy their job as watchmen of the rainforest.

Environmental Change Effects:

Environmental change represents a huge danger to rainforests and the networks subject to them. Changes in precipitation designs, climbing temperatures, and outrageous climate occasions can disturb conventional natural information and asset the board rehearses. Native people group should adjust to these progressions while fighting with the more extensive effects of a warming planet.

4. Native Opposition and Preservation Drives:

Land Freedoms Support:

Native people group are at the very front of upholding for their property freedoms. Developments for land privileges acknowledgment have picked up speed worldwide, with native pioneers and activists attempting to get lawful securities for their domains. The acknowledgment of land freedoms isn't just a question of equity yet a basic move toward engaging native guardianship.

Local area drove Protection Ventures:

Numerous native networks start and lead their preservation projects, consolidating customary information with current logical methodologies. These ventures frequently center around environment rebuilding, reasonable asset the board, and local area instruction. By effectively taking part in protection drives, native people groups show their obligation to saving the rainforest for people in the future.

Worldwide Joint effort:

Native people group take part in worldwide joint efforts with natural associations, specialists, and policymakers to enhance their voices on the worldwide stage. These coordinated efforts encourage the trading of information, assets, and procedures for rainforest preservation. Native drove drives benefit from the help of the worldwide local area, building up the interconnectedness of preservation endeavors.

****5. Examples of overcoming adversity in Native Rainforest Protection:**

The Kayapo of the Brazilian Amazon:

The Kayapo nation in the Brazilian Amazon have been effective in opposing area infringement and upholding for their privileges. Through associations with natural associations, they have executed manageable advancement projects, safeguarded their domains from criminal operations, and kept up with their conventional practices while adding to rainforest preservation.

The Penan of Borneo:

The Penan, native to Borneo, have for some time been safeguards of their rainforest homes. Confronting dangers from logging and palm oil businesses, they have participated in fights in court and direct activities to safeguard their regions. The Penan's strength and obligation to protection feature the capability of native networks to oppose outer tensions.

The Achuar of the Amazon Bowl:

The Achuar public, dwelling in the Amazon Bowl, have created local area based preservation drives to safeguard their tribal terrains. Their endeavors incorporate economical asset the board, ecotourism adventures, and associations with protection associations. The Achuar exhibit how native information can illuminate fruitful preservation methodologies.

****6. Enabling Native Guardianship for What's to come:**

Legitimate Acknowledgment of Land Privileges:

Guaranteeing the legitimate acknowledgment of native land privileges is a basic move toward enabling their guardianship. State run administrations and worldwide bodies should maintain the standards of free, earlier, and informed assent, recognizing the independence of native networks in dealing with their regions. Lawful structures ought to safeguard native grounds from infringement and abuse.

Interest in Manageable Occupations:

Supporting manageable occupations for native networks is significant for their proceeded with guardianship. Interests in eco-accommodating monetary exercises, for example, agroforestry, non-wood backwoods items, and local area based the travel industry, give options in contrast to horrendous enterprises. These drives add to nearby economies while building up the worth of flawless rainforest biological systems.

Social Protection and Training:

Saving native societies is indistinguishable from rainforest preservation. Endeavors to archive, revive, and send conventional information to more youthful ages guarantee the congruity of manageable practices. Training programs that incorporate both customary and logical information engage native youth to be powerful stewards of their genealogical grounds.

Worldwide Help and Fortitude:

The worldwide local area should effectively support and stand in fortitude with native watchmen. This includes pushing for their freedoms, bringing issues to light about the dangers they face, and supporting protection drives drove by native networks. Worldwide joint efforts ought to focus on the voices and needs of native people groups in molding worldwide protection procedures.

****7. Looking Forward: A Common Obligation:**

As the gatekeepers of the rainforest, native networks hold a remarkable and indispensable job in the preservation of these fundamental environments. Their conventional information, feasible practices, and profound association with the land add to the flexibility of rainforest biological systems. Notwithstanding, the difficulties they face require aggregate activity and a reconsideration of worldwide needs.

Looking forward, the safeguarding of rainforests requires a change in perspective that perceives the natural worth of native guardianship. It includes recognizing the interconnectedness of environmental, social, and social frameworks. Rainforest preservation shouldn't just focus on the insurance of biodiversity yet additionally maintain the freedoms, independence, and prosperity of the native people groups who act as its stewards.

The eventual fate of rainforest protection lies in cooperative endeavors that span conventional insight with contemporary science, engage native networks, and address the main drivers of deforestation and double-dealing. As the world wrestles with natural emergencies, the guardianship of the rainforest by native networks remains as an encouraging sign, helping us to remember the basic to safeguard the World's most different and delicate biological systems for a long time into the future.

4.1Exploration of the role of Sumatran tigers as keystone species in maintaining the ecological balance of the rainforest.

The rainforests of Sumatra are not only wealthy in biodiversity; they are likewise perplexing environments where every species assumes an essential part in keeping up with the sensitive equilibrium of nature. Among the heap of verdure, the Sumatran tiger (Panthera tigris sumatrae) stands apart as a cornerstone animal groups, standing firm on an exceptional and fundamental footing in the biological embroidery of the rainforest. This investigation digs into the multi-layered job of Sumatran tigers as cornerstone species, unwinding their effect on the environment, their collaborations with different species, and the ramifications for the general soundness of the rainforest.

**1. Characterizing Cornerstone Species:

Biological Specialists:

Cornerstone species are living beings that apply an unbalanced effect on the design and working of a biological system. Their presence or nonappearance can have flowing impacts, molding the overflow and variety of different species. Cornerstone species are in many cases thought about biological designers, as they assume a focal part in keeping up with the equilibrium of the environment.

Top Hunters in Environments:

In numerous environments, top hunters like the Sumatran tiger go about as cornerstone species. These hunters control prey populaces, forestall overgrazing, and impact the way of behaving of different species in the food web. The evacuation of a cornerstone animal types can prompt irregular characteristics, influencing the whole environment.

**2. The Remarkable Job of Sumatran Tigers:

Top Carnivores in the Natural pecking order:

Sumatran tigers, being dominant hunters, possess the most noteworthy trophic level in the rainforest established pecking order. As carnivores, they fundamentally go after ungulates like deer and wild hog. The guideline of herbivore populaces by tigers significantly affects vegetation, forestalling unreasonable perusing and keeping up with the soundness of plant networks.

Impact on Prey Conduct:

The presence of Sumatran tigers impacts the way of behaving of their prey. Ungulates modify their taking care of examples, stay away from specific regions, and show elevated cautiousness because of the danger of predation. These conduct changes significantly affect vegetation, impacting plant structure and circulation.

Regional Elements:

Sumatran tigers are regional creatures, and their domains frequently envelop huge regions inside the rainforest. The foundation of domains controls the appropriation of prey species, forestalling overexploitation in unambiguous locales. The regional elements of tigers add to spatial heterogeneity in the environment.

**3. Forestalling Overgrazing and Herbivore Populace Control:

Controlling Ungulate Populaces:

Sumatran tigers assume an essential part in controlling the populaces of herbivores in the rainforest. By going after ungulates, they forestall overgrazing, guaranteeing a harmony among herbivore and plant populaces. This guideline is imperative for the upkeep of assorted vegetation and the avoidance of territory debasement.

Influence on Plant Recovery:

The control of herbivore populaces by Sumatran tigers upgrades the recovery of plant species. In regions where tigers are dynamic, the decreased perusing pressure permits plant seedlings to flourish, adding to the variety and design of the rainforest. This, thusly, upholds various different organic entities reliant upon solid vegetation.

****4. Keeping up with Biodiversity:**

Saving Species Variety:

The presence of cornerstone species like the Sumatran tiger adds to the general biodiversity of the rainforest. By controlling prey populaces, tigers forestall the predominance of specific species and make conditions for a different cluster of plants and creatures to coincide. Biodiversity is vital for the strength and flexibility of biological systems despite ecological changes.

Influence on Mesopredators:

Sumatran tigers likewise impact the populaces of mesopredators (mid-level hunters) in the rainforest. The concealment of mesopredator populaces by tigers keeps these more modest hunters from applying unjustifiable strain on their own prey species. This various leveled guideline keeps a reasonable local area of hunters and prey.

****5. Seed Dispersal and Timberland Recovery:**

Seed Dispersal by Tigers:

While principally carnivores, Sumatran tigers accidentally add to seed dispersal. The undigested seeds in their dung are kept across their domains as they travel through the rainforest. This cycle works with the colonization of new plant species in various regions, adding to hereditary variety and the recovery of the timberland.

Making Environment Mosaics:

The development of tigers across their domains makes living space mosaics with differing levels of vegetation thickness. This spatial heterogeneity helps a great many animal categories, as various plants and creatures flourish in various territories. The mosaic impact adds to the general versatility and flexibility of the rainforest environment.

****6. Human-Untamed life Struggle Relief:**

Adjusting Human-Untamed life Cooperations:

The presence of Sumatran tigers in the rainforest can assist with adjusting cooperations among people and untamed life. By directing the populaces of herbivores, tigers lessen the probability of harvest attacking by ungulates and alleviate clashes between neighborhood networks and natural life. This, thus, encourages conjunction and decreases the tensions on both human and tiger populaces.

Eco-the travel industry Potential open doors:

The charming idea of Sumatran tigers presents potential open doors for eco-the travel industry, giving monetary motivations to nearby networks to save these cornerstone hunters.

Capable eco-the travel industry can produce income that upholds preservation endeavors, advances mindfulness, and supports the benefit of keeping up with in one piece rainforest environments.

7. Difficulties and Protection Concerns:

Territory Misfortune and Fracture:

The essential danger to Sumatran tigers is territory misfortune and fracture because of human exercises. Deforestation for farming, logging, and framework improvement infringes upon tiger living spaces, prompting secluded populaces and expanded weakness to outer tensions.

Poaching and Unlawful Untamed life Exchange:

Poaching for the unlawful untamed life exchange, driven by interest for tiger parts and items, stays a huge danger. Notwithstanding preservation endeavors and against poaching measures, Sumatran tigers face the persevering gamble of being focused on for their skins, bones, and other body parts.

Environmental Change Effect:

Environmental change represents a danger to the rainforest biological systems that Sumatran tigers call home. Modified precipitation designs, increasing temperatures, and other environment related changes can affect the accessibility of prey species, upset territory appropriateness, and posture difficulties to the versatile limit of the two tigers and their biological systems.

8. Protection Techniques for Sumatran Tigers:

Territory Security and Rebuilding:

Integral to the preservation of Sumatran tigers is the security and rebuilding of their natural surroundings. Laying out and really overseeing safeguarded regions, as well as reestablishing debased natural surroundings, are fundamental for guaranteeing the accessibility of reasonable domains for tiger populaces.

Hostile to Poaching and Policing:

Fortifying enemy of poaching endeavors and upgrading policing basic parts of Sumatran tiger protection. Preparing and preparing officers, utilizing progressed reconnaissance innovations, and encouraging global joint effort add to lessening the danger of poaching.

Local area Commitment and Work Backing:

Drawing in nearby networks as accomplices in tiger preservation is vital. Supporting feasible livelihoods, integrating nearby information into preservation methodologies, and cultivating a feeling of responsibility and pride in tiger protection add to the progress of protection drives.

Transboundary Cooperation:

Sumatran tigers don't perceive political lines, and their protection requires transboundary cooperation. Coordination between various locales, global associations, and adjoining nations is crucial for address the mind boggling difficulties confronting tiger populaces.

Environment Versatile Preservation Techniques:

Environment versatile preservation techniques consider the likely effects of environmental change on Sumatran tiger living spaces and prey species. Versatile administration draws near, informed by continuous exploration and checking, can help moderates expect and answer environment related difficulties.

4.2Highlighting the symbiotic relationship between Sumatran tigers and their environment.

In the core of the lavish rainforests of Sumatra, a dazzling dance unfurls — one that entwines the lofty Sumatran tiger (Panthera tigris sumatrae) with the mind boggling trap of life in its current circumstance. This harmonious relationship isn't just an organic interaction however a dynamic and sensitive embroidery that winds around together the endurance of the tiger, the strength of the rainforest, and the prosperity of the innumerable species that call this lively biological system home. This investigation dives into the subtleties of this advantageous relationship, revealing insight into the shared conditions, biological jobs, and protection suggestions that emerge from the agreeable dance between Sumatran tigers and their current circumstance.

****1. The Tiger's Space: A Sanctuary in the Rainforest:**

The Rainforest as Living space:

The rainforests of Sumatra furnish the Sumatran tiger with a huge and changed environment. These thick and biodiverse environments, portrayed by transcending trees, lavish vegetation, and wandering streams, offer the ideal material for the tiger's cryptic and single way of life. The tiger's natural surroundings stretches out from marsh woodlands to montane regions, displaying its flexibility to different conditions inside the rainforest.

Regional Elements:

Sumatran tigers are regional animals, with every individual guaranteeing a critical scope of the rainforest just like own. These domains act as both hunting grounds and reproducing regions, furnishing the tiger with the space it requirements to satisfy its natural job as a top hunter.

The regional elements of tigers add to the spatial heterogeneity of the rainforest, making an interwoven of environments that upholds a different scope of animal varieties.

****2. Cornerstone Hunters: Molding the Biological system:**

Managing Prey Populaces:

At the summit of the pecking order, Sumatran tigers employ huge impact over their prey. Ungulates like deer and wild pig structure the essential eating regimen of tigers, and their predation serves a significant natural job. By directing the populaces of herbivores, tigers forestall overgrazing and keep up with the strength of vegetation in the rainforest. This command over herbivore populaces shapes the actual organization of plant networks.

Controlling Mesopredators:

Past their immediate effect on prey species, tigers assume a part in controlling mesopredators — mid-level hunters — in the rainforest. The presence of tigers stifles the populaces of more modest hunters like panthers and dholes, keeping them from applying unnecessary tension on their own prey species. This progressive guideline adds to the equilibrium of hunter prey connections.

3. The Dance of Concurrence: Different Species in the Tiger's Domain:

Biodiversity Area of interest:

The rainforests of Sumatra are perceived as worldwide biodiversity areas of interest, facilitating a dumbfounding exhibit of plant and creature species. Inside the tiger's domain, this biodiversity isn't simply a fortuitous event yet a result of the tiger's job as a cornerstone animal groups. By keeping a reasonable biological system, tigers encourage conditions helpful for the concurrence of different widely varied vegetation.

Unintentional Landscapers:

The tiger's impact reaches out past predation. As tigers cross their domains, they accidentally add to the dispersal of seeds. The undigested seeds in their excrement track down new homes across the rainforest, working with the recovery of plant species. In this accidental job as grounds-keepers, tigers become fundamental to the repetitive cycles of woodland recovery.

4. Seed Dispersal: An Inconspicuous Commitment to Backwoods Wellbeing:

Releasing Life:

The tiger's part in seed dispersal is an unpretentious yet significant commitment to the wellbeing and essentialness of the rainforest. As seeds go through the tiger's stomach related framework, they are a saved across its area. This cycle, known as endozoochory, releases the potential for new life in various region of the rainforest. The places where seeds are stored become focal points for plant recovery.

Hereditary Variety and Variation:

Past the actual demonstration of seed dispersal, tigers likewise assume a part in the hereditary variety and transformation of plant species. The development of tigers across enormous regions guarantees that seeds are conveyed over a wide geographic reach, upgrading the hereditary variety of plant populaces. This variety is critical for the versatility and flexibility of plant networks even with natural changes.

5. Human-Tiger Elements: Adjusting Concurrence:

Human-Untamed life Struggle Moderation:

The presence of Sumatran tigers in the rainforest has suggestions for human-untamed life elements. While tigers are frequently tricky and will quite often stay away from direct contact with people, clashes can emerge, especially in regions where human exercises converge with tiger domains. Relieving human-natural life struggle turns into a pivotal part of protection, requiring procedures that balance the necessities of neighborhood networks with the conservation of tiger living spaces.

Eco-The travel industry Open doors:

The mystique and appeal of Sumatran tigers present open doors for eco-the travel industry drives. Dependable eco-the travel industry can produce income for nearby networks, giving monetary impetuses to the preservation of tiger territories. The income created can uphold preservation endeavors, encourage local area commitment, and add to the general prosperity of the two tigers and neighborhood populaces.

**6. Protection Difficulties and Methodologies:

Territory Misfortune and Fracture:

The essential danger to the advantageous connection between Sumatran tigers and their current circumstance is natural surroundings misfortune and fracture. Deforestation for farming, logging, and foundation improvement infringes upon tiger environments, prompting confined populaces and expanded weakness to outer tensions. Preservation procedures should focus on the security and reclamation of tiger territories.

Poaching and Unlawful Untamed life Exchange:

Poaching for the unlawful untamed life exchange represents a relentless danger to Sumatran tigers. The interest for tiger parts and items drives unlawful hunting, in spite of endeavors to check this exchange. Against poaching measures, policing, worldwide cooperation are pivotal parts of preservation procedures pointed toward shielding tigers from the danger of poaching.

Environmental Change Effect:

Environmental change presents an extra layer of intricacy to the protection condition. Changes in precipitation designs, climbing temperatures, and other environment related effects can modify the dissemination of prey species, influence natural surroundings appropriateness, and posture difficulties to the versatile limit of the two tigers and their biological systems. Environment tough protection procedures are fundamental for tending to these difficulties.

**7. Concordance in Protection: Sustaining the Dance of Advantageous interaction:

All encompassing Preservation Approaches:

The preservation of Sumatran tigers and their cooperative relationship with the rainforest requests comprehensive methodologies that rise above conventional limits. Endeavors should envelop living space insurance, hostile to poaching measures, local area commitment, and environment strong systems. Incorporated preservation designs that address the interconnected difficulties looked by tigers and their current circumstance are fundamental.

Local area Strengthening:

Drawing in neighborhood networks as stewards of the rainforest is essential to the outcome of preservation endeavors. Enabling people group through practical vocations, training, and participatory preservation drives cultivates a feeling of obligation and possession. The prosperity of the two tigers and people relies on an amicable concurrence that regards the necessities of both.

Global Joint effort:

Sumatran tigers don't perceive political lines, and their protection requires global coordinated effort. Facilitated endeavors between states, protection associations, and nearby networks can enhance the effect of preservation drives. Sharing information, assets, and best practices on a worldwide scale builds up the interconnectedness of protection endeavors.

****8. Looking Forward: Supporting the Dance for A long time into the future:**

In the dance between Sumatran tigers and their current circumstance, the means are mind boggling, the rhythms complex, and the congruity fragile. As we look forward, the fate of this advantageous relationship rests in our grasp. Sustaining this dance requires not just a pledge to the protection of a charming animal categories yet a significant comprehension of the interconnectedness that characterizes the rainforest biological system.

In the embroidery of nature, where each string is woven into the texture of life, Sumatran tigers arise as gatekeepers of biodiversity and stewards of the rainforest's wellbeing. As we endeavor to safeguard these puzzling animals, we set out on an excursion that goes past the endurance of a solitary animal types. It is an excursion toward defending the strength of environments, advancing concurrence among people and natural life, and guaranteeing that the dance of beneficial interaction go on for a long time into the future. The rainforests of Sumatra, with their magnetic tigers, entice us to join this dance — a dance that holds the commitment of an amicable and feasible future for the rich embroidery of life on The planet.

Chapter 5

Conservation Efforts

Preservation endeavors assume an essential part in shielding the sensitive equilibrium of environments, protecting biodiversity, and guaranteeing the manageability of our planet for people in the future. As the worldwide populace keeps on developing, human exercises apply expanding tension on the climate, prompting living space annihilation, loss of biodiversity, and environmental change. Because of these difficulties, protection endeavors have arisen as a basic part of natural stewardship. This complete investigation dives into the different features of protection, going from the verifiable setting to contemporary drives, and features the significance of individual and aggregate activities in relieving the effect of human exercises on the normal world.

Authentic Point of view:

The underlying foundations of preservation endeavors can be followed back to early human advancements where networks perceived the need to oversee normal assets for their food. Old practices, like controlled consuming and rotational brushing, exhibited a natural comprehension of environmental elements. In any case, it was only after the nineteenth century that the cutting edge preservation development came to fruition, powered by worries over deforestation, natural life exhaustion, and the infringement of industrialization.

One of the original figures throughout the entire existence of protection is John Muir, a Scottish-American naturalist and promoter for the safeguarding of wild in the US. Muir's endeavors prompted the foundation of the Sierra Club in 1892, an association that assumed a crucial part in the formation of public parks and the improvement of natural strategies. Simultaneously, Theodore Roosevelt, the 26th Leader of the US, contributed altogether to the preservation cause by extending the public park framework and making the US Backwoods Administration.

The mid-twentieth century saw the rise of worldwide mindfulness with respect to natural issues. The distribution of Rachel Carson's pivotal book, "Quiet Spring," in 1962, uncovered the impeding impacts of pesticides, igniting another rush of ecological cognizance. The 1970s denoted the initiation of Earth Day and the foundation of ecological security organizations around the world, establishing the groundwork for contemporary preservation endeavors.

Biodiversity Preservation:

Biodiversity, the assortment of life on The planet, is a basic part of sound environments. Preservation endeavors center around shielding this variety, perceiving the interconnectedness of species and the environment administrations they give. Safeguarded regions, for example, public parks and natural life saves, act as safe-havens for a horde of animal groups, giving a shelter from living space obliteration, poaching, and other anthropogenic dangers.

The Worldwide Association for Protection of Nature (IUCN) Red Rundown is an exhaustive information base that surveys the eradication chance of thousands of species. It fills in as an important device for traditionalists and policymakers to focus on their endeavors. Species recuperation programs, hostage rearing drives, and natural surroundings rebuilding projects are necessary parts of biodiversity preservation.

Besides, the Show on Natural Variety (CBD), laid out in 1992, is a worldwide settlement that expects to monitor biodiversity, guarantee supportable utilization of organic assets, and advance the fair and evenhanded sharing of advantages got from hereditary assets. The CBD's essential objectives, known as the Aichi Targets, give a system to worldwide endeavors to end biodiversity misfortune.

Natural surroundings Reclamation:

Natural surroundings obliteration, driven by urbanization, farming, and asset extraction, represents a critical danger to biodiversity. Preservation endeavors progressively center around living space rebuilding as a way to moderate the effect of human exercises. Reclamation projects include restoring local vegetation, making untamed life passages, and resuscitating debased biological systems.

Reforestation drives, for example, the Bonn Challenge, plan to reestablish 350 million hectares of deforested and debased land by 2030. Trees assume a urgent part in carbon sequestration, soil adjustment, and giving living space to endless species. The significance of mangrove rebuilding is additionally earning respect, given the crucial job mangroves play in beach front biological systems, going about as nurseries for fish and giving security against tempests and disintegration.

Notwithstanding earthly territories, oceanic environments are a focal point of rebuilding endeavors. Coral reefs, fundamental for marine biodiversity, face dangers from environmental change, overfishing, and contamination. Coral rebuilding projects include strategies, for example, coral cultivating and transplantation to restore corrupted reefs and upgrade their strength to ecological stressors.

Environmental Change Relief:

Environmental change addresses one of the most squeezing difficulties to worldwide preservation endeavors. The expansion in ozone depleting substance outflows, principally from human exercises, adds to climbing temperatures, ocean level ascent, and outrageous climate occasions. Preservation methodologies progressively integrate environmental change relief and transformation measures to address these difficulties.

Environmentally friendly power drives, for example, sun oriented and wind power, assume a vital part in diminishing fossil fuel byproducts. The progress from petroleum products to practical energy sources is a critical part of worldwide endeavors to battle environmental change. Traditionalists advocate for the security of carbon-rich biological systems like backwoods and peatlands, which go about as carbon sinks, engrossing and putting away a lot of carbon dioxide.

Moreover, supportable land-use rehearses, for example, agroforestry and regenerative agribusiness, advance carbon sequestration in soils and add to environment flexibility. Safeguarded regions likewise act as cushions against the effects of environmental change, giving living spaces that permit species to move and adjust to evolving conditions.

Preservation and Native Information:

Native people group have long assumed a vital part in the preservation of biodiversity. Their conventional information, went down through ages, offers important bits of knowledge into maintainable asset the board and environment versatility. Perceiving the significance of native viewpoints, protection endeavors progressively embrace cooperative methodologies that include neighborhood networks in dynamic cycles.

Native Safeguarded and Rationed Regions (IPCAs) are acquiring unmistakable quality as a model for protection that regards conventional information and encourages local area stewardship. These regions, oversaw by native networks, contribute not exclusively to biodiversity protection yet additionally to the conservation of social legacy and the advancement of practical occupations.

Difficulties and Reactions:

Regardless of huge advancement, protection endeavors face various difficulties and reactions. Lacking subsidizing, insufficient authorization of ecological guidelines, and the continuous loss of regular natural surroundings keep on undermining biodiversity. The inconsistent appropriation of preservation benefits and the relocation of neighborhood networks from safeguarded regions raise moral worries.

Besides, pundits contend that customary preservation approaches have once in a while overlooked the privileges and needs of neighborhood networks, prompting clashes and sabotaging the viability of protection drives.

Adjusting the conservation of biological systems with the financial necessities of networks requires a nuanced and comprehensive methodology.

The Job of Innovation in Preservation:

Progressions in innovation have upset protection endeavors, giving devices to observing, exploration, and information examination. Satellite symbolism and remote detecting empower researchers to follow changes in land cover, deforestation, and natural life populaces on a worldwide scale. Drones offer a savvy and productive method for looking over huge regions and checking hard-to-arrive at areas.

The utilization of camera traps and acoustic checking gadgets has changed untamed life research, permitting researchers to assemble information on subtle and nighttime species. Protectionists influence information examination and computerized reasoning to process and dissect huge measures of data, supporting species recognizable proof, environment planning, and the improvement of prescient models.

Innovation likewise assumes a basic part in enemy of poaching endeavors. The utilization of brilliant watching, GPS following, and the sending of sensor networks in safeguarded regions improve the capacity to distinguish and answer criminal operations. Traditionalists are progressively investigating the capability of arising advancements, for example, blockchain, to battle natural life dealing with by further developing straightforwardness supply chains and reinforcing policing.

Preservation and Practical Turn of events:

The connection among preservation and supportable improvement is an intricate and dynamic transaction. While preservation endeavors customarily centered around safeguarding unblemished wild, there is a developing acknowledgment of the need to incorporate protection objectives with more extensive improvement goals. Reasonable improvement looks to adjust monetary, social, and natural contemplations, recognizing the interconnectedness of these aspects.

Preservation drives that line up with manageable advancement standards intend to make mutual benefit situations, where biodiversity protection improves environment administrations, upholds nearby jobs, and adds to neediness easing. Ecotourism, for instance, addresses a feasible monetary model that produces income for preservation while giving business open doors to neighborhood networks.

The idea of Installments for Environment Administrations (PES) is one more creative methodology that perceives the worth of normal assets and the administrations they give. In PES projects, people or elements pay for the protection and economical administration of biological systems that add to clean water, carbon sequestration, and other fundamental administrations.

Local area Based Preservation:

Local area based preservation approaches engage nearby networks to take part in the administration and security of regular assets effectively. Perceiving the conventional information and practices of native people groups, these drives cultivate a feeling of pride and obligation among local area individuals.

Local area based preservation frequently includes the foundation of local area oversaw saves, where nearby networks start to lead the pack in dynamic cycles and advantage straightforwardly from the protection of biodiversity. This approach tends to the requirements of neighborhood networks as well as improves the adequacy and supportability of preservation endeavors.

Schooling and Mindfulness:

Public mindfulness and training are fundamental parts of fruitful preservation endeavors. Building a worldwide comprehension of the significance of biodiversity, biological systems, and the effect of human exercises on the climate is essential for encouraging an aggregate obligation to preservation.

Ecological training programs in schools, outreach drives, and missions by non-administrative associations (NGOs) add to bringing issues to light about protection issues. Drawing in the general population in resident science projects, where people add to information assortment and observing endeavors, makes a feeling of association and obligation.

The Job of States and Worldwide Participation:

Legislatures assume a focal part in molding and carrying out preservation strategies. The foundation and the executives of safeguarded regions, requirement of natural guidelines, and the designation of subsidizing for preservation drives fall inside the domain of administrative organizations.

Worldwide participation is foremost in tending to worldwide natural difficulties. Deals and arrangements, like the Show on Organic Variety (CBD), the Paris Settlement on environmental change, and the Ramsar Show on wetlands, give structures to cooperative activity. Global endeavors are fundamental for tending to transboundary issues, for example, transitory species preservation and the guideline of exercises that influence shared biological systems.

Examples of overcoming adversity and Protection Wins:

In the midst of the difficulties, there are striking examples of overcoming adversity that feature the viability of protection endeavors. The recuperation of specific species from the edge of annihilation, like the bald eagle and the California condor, exhibits the positive effect of designated preservation mediations.

Protection achievement is additionally clear in the resurgence of biological systems following rebuilding endeavors. The renewed introduction of wolves to Yellowstone Public Park in the US, for instance, prompted an outpouring of environmental advantages, including the recovery of vegetation and the adjustment of riverbanks.

5.1 Overview of ongoing conservation initiatives and projects aimed at protecting Sumatran tigers.

Sumatra, the 6th biggest island on the planet, is prestigious for its rich biodiversity, facilitating a horde of exceptional and jeopardized species. Among these, the Sumatran tiger (Panthera tigris sumatrae) stands apart as an image of the island's environmental significance. Notwithstanding, this lofty enormous feline appearances extreme dangers to its endurance, essentially because of environment misfortune, human-untamed life struggle, and unlawful poaching. Because of these difficulties, different protection drives and tasks have been started to shield the eventual fate of Sumatran tigers. This complete outline will dive into the continuous endeavors pointed toward safeguarding these jeopardized cats, investigating the procedures utilized, challenges confronted, and the effect of these preservation tries.

1. **Foundation on Sumatran Tigers**

   Prior to diving into preservation drives, understanding the basic environmental and organic parts of Sumatran tigers is fundamental. The Sumatran tiger is the littlest of all tiger subspecies and is solely tracked down on the Indonesian island of Sumatra. It is assessed that a couple hundred people stay in the wild, making it one of the most extraordinary and most imperiled large felines universally. Sumatran tigers are adjusted to different natural surroundings, going from swamp woodlands to hilly districts, however they are especially powerless against living space discontinuity and misfortune.

2. **Significant Dangers to Sumatran Tigers**

1. **Territory Misfortune and Discontinuity:**

   One of the essential dangers to Sumatran tigers is the continuous misfortune and fracture of their regular living space. Fast deforestation, driven by rural extension, logging, and foundation advancement, has brought about segregated pockets of tiger populaces. This fracture makes it hard for tigers to track down mates, prompting diminished hereditary variety and an expanded gamble of inbreeding.

2. **Human-Natural life Struggle:**

   As human populaces venture into tiger environments, clashes among people and tigers raise. Tigers might go after domesticated animals, prompting retaliatory killings by nearby networks.

   This contention not just represents an immediate danger to individual tigers yet in addition adds to negative view of these creatures, further endangering their preservation.

3. **Unlawful Poaching:**

Poaching for the unlawful untamed life exchange, driven by interest for tiger parts and items, stays a critical danger. Sumatran tigers are pursued for their skin, bones, and other body parts, which are utilized in conventional Asian medication and as extravagance things. Regardless of worldwide endeavors to battle natural life dealing, the unlawful exchange tiger parts perseveres, coming down on currently weak populaces.

III. Protection Drives and Ventures

1. **Safeguarded Regions and Territory Rebuilding:**

   To address territory misfortune and fracture, different preservation associations and administrative bodies have laid out safeguarded regions and public parks committed to the protection of Sumatran tigers. These regions act as imperative shelters for the tigers, giving undisturbed environments where they can meander, chase, and recreate. Also, living space rebuilding projects expect to restore corrupted scenes, making network between divided regions.

2. **Local area Based Protection:**
   Perceiving the significance of neighborhood networks in tiger preservation, a few undertakings embrace a local area based approach. This includes drawing in with and enabling nearby networks to become dynamic members in tiger preservation endeavors. Drives might incorporate schooling programs, elective work improvement, and the foundation of local area oversaw saves that balance the requirements of the two individuals and tigers.

3. **Hostile to Poaching Measures:**
   In the fight against unlawful poaching, hostile to poaching units and policing team up to fortify watching and reconnaissance endeavors. This incorporates the utilization of current innovation, for example, camera traps, robots, and satellite following to screen tiger populaces and distinguish likely dangers. Moreover, global joint effort and stricter requirement of untamed life dealing regulations add to upsetting the unlawful exchange organization.

4. **Exploration and Observing:**
   Progressing research drives center around grasping the biology, conduct, and soundness of Sumatran tigers. This information is pivotal for planning powerful protection techniques. Observing projects utilize a blend of field studies, camera catching, and hereditary examination to follow populace patterns, survey the effect of protection mediations, and illuminate versatile administration draws near.

5. **Movement and Hereditary Administration:**

To address the difficulties of divided territories and inbreeding, some protection projects investigate movement techniques. This includes moving tigers from secluded populaces to lay out or reinforce populaces in other reasonable regions. Hereditary administration plans are likewise carried out to guarantee the upkeep of hereditary variety inside populaces, decreasing the gamble of hereditary problems and upgrading the drawn out practicality of the species.

IV. Examples of overcoming adversity and Positive Results

In spite of the considerable difficulties confronting Sumatran tiger preservation, a few drives have exhibited positive results.

1. **Expansion in Tiger Populaces:**
   In specific safeguarded regions, purposeful protection endeavors have prompted an expansion in Sumatran tiger populaces. This shows the viability of systems, for example, territory security, hostile to poaching measures, and local area association.

2. **Diminished Human-Untamed life Struggle:**
   Local area based protection programs have effectively relieved human-natural life clashes by executing estimates, for example, secure domesticated animals

lodging, early admonition frameworks, and pay plans for domesticated animals misfortunes. These drives encourage uplifting outlooks toward tigers among neighborhood networks, cultivating conjunction.

3. **Global Cooperation:**

Cooperative endeavors between legislative offices, non-administrative associations (NGOs), and worldwide bodies have fortified the battle against unlawful natural life dealing. Global tension and participation have prompted expanded implementation, stricter punishments, and the destroying of untamed life dealing organizations.

V. Challenges and Remaining Worries

1. **Restricted Subsidizing:**
   In spite of the positive steps, subsidizing stays a tenacious test for the majority protection drives. Restricted monetary assets upset the scale and viability of preservation projects, making it urgent to get supported help from states, NGOs, and global givers.

2. **Political Will and Administration:**
   The progress of preservation endeavors is in many cases dependent upon political will and successful administration. In certain areas, feeble requirement of ecological regulations, debasement, and clashing advancement plans keep on subverting preservation drives.

3. **Environmental Change Effect:**
   The speeding up impacts of environmental change represent an extra danger to Sumatran tigers and their living spaces. Changes in temperature, precipitation designs, and the recurrence of outrageous climate occasions can disturb environments, modify prey accessibility, and fuel existing difficulties.

4. **Poaching and Unlawful Exchange:**

Regardless of escalated enemy of poaching endeavors, the unlawful exchange tiger parts endures. Coordinated criminal organizations associated with untamed life dealing adjust to implementation measures, featuring the requirement for proceeded with advancement and joint effort in fighting this worthwhile exchange.

VI. Future Headings and Proposals

1. **Fortifying Worldwide Collaboration:**
   Given the transboundary idea of protection issues, it is crucial for encourage global joint effort. Joint endeavors including state run administrations, NGOs, and global bodies can improve the trading of information, assets, and ability to on the whole address difficulties.

2. **Putting resources into Instruction and Mindfulness:**
   Long haul protection achievement requires building mindfulness and

encouraging a feeling of obligation among neighborhood networks. Training programs focused on schools, networks, and the overall population can impart a more profound comprehension of the significance of biodiversity and the job every individual plays in preservation.

3. **Integrating Native Information:**
   Incorporating native information and conventional practices into preservation methodologies can enhance the comprehension of biological systems and add to economical conjunction between nearby networks and untamed life.

4. **Adjusting to Environmental Change:**
   Environmental change strength ought to be integrated into protection arranging. This includes distinguishing and carrying out techniques to assist the two tigers and their territories with adjusting to changing natural circumstances.

5. **Advancing Economical Turn of events:**

Offsetting preservation with maintainable improvement is significant for the drawn out progress of Sumatran tiger protection. Executing eco-accommodating works on, supporting manageable vocations, and integrating protection contemplations into land-use arranging add to this sensitive equilibrium.

5.2 Discussion on the involvement of local communities, NGOs, and governmental organizations in these efforts.

The preservation of Sumatran tigers is a diverse test that requests the dynamic inclusion of different partners. Among the vital participants are neighborhood networks, non-administrative associations (NGOs), and legislative associations, each contributing extraordinary points of view, assets, and endeavors to protect the fate of these jeopardized enormous felines. This conversation investigates the urgent jobs played by these elements in continuous protection drives, featuring their commitments, challenges confronted, and the significance of cooperative endeavors.

1. **Neighborhood People group in Tiger Protection**
1. **Grasping Neighborhood Points of view:**
   Nearby people group living in and around tiger environments are vital to preservation endeavors. Their points of view, information on the scene, and conventional practices add to an all encompassing comprehension of the environment. Drives that draw in with nearby networks look to consolidate their bits of knowledge, guaranteeing that protection procedures line up with the requirements and yearnings of individuals who share their living space with these wonderful animals.

2. **Local area Based Preservation:**
   Perceiving that fruitful protection relies on the help of neighborhood occupants, local area based preservation projects have acquired noticeable quality. These ventures mean to enable networks to become stewards of their normal

environmental elements.

This includes training programs, ability advancement, and elective job open doors that lessen reliance on exercises adverse to tiger environments, like logging or impractical farming.

3. **Moderating Human-Untamed life Struggle:**
   Nearby people group frequently face difficulties emerging from human-untamed life struggle, particularly when tigers go after animals. Preservation drives work connected at the hip with these networks to execute measures like secure animals lodging, early admonition frameworks, and remuneration for misfortunes. By tending to these worries, protectionists construct positive associations with neighborhood occupants, cultivating a feeling of shared liability regarding the conjunction of people and tigers.

4. **Native Information and Preservation:**
   The rich native information on nearby networks is a significant resource in preservation endeavors. Conventional practices that advance concordance with nature, economical asset the board, and untamed life protection are incorporated into preservation methodologies. This upgrades the viability of drives as well as regards and jam the social legacy of neighborhood networks.

5. **Local area Oversaw Stores:**

Some preservation projects empower the foundation of local area oversaw saves, where nearby occupants effectively take part in the security and checking of tiger territories. These stores act as a model for reasonable preservation, showing the positive effect of cooperative endeavors among protectionists and individuals who call these districts home.

II. Non-Legislative Associations (NGOs) in Tiger Preservation

1. **Executing Preservation Drives:**
   NGOs assume a urgent part in executing on-the-ground preservation drives. Their dexterity, adaptability, and mastery make them appropriate to address explicit difficulties looked by Sumatran tigers. NGOs frequently team up with nearby networks, administrative associations, and worldwide bodies to plan and execute designated programs that address the main drivers of tiger decline.

2. **Raising support and Asset Activation:**
   One of the basic elements of NGOs is raising money to help preservation projects. Through associations with worldwide givers, corporate backers, and individual patrons, NGOs secure the monetary assets expected for research, living space assurance, against poaching endeavors, and local area commitment. These assets are instrumental in crossing over holes in government subsidizing and guaranteeing the coherence of long haul preservation drives.

3. **Exploration and Development:**
NGOs are at the front of logical exploration and advancement in the field of tiger preservation. They put resources into advancements, for example, camera traps, satellite following, and hereditary examination to accumulate urgent information on tiger populaces, conduct, and wellbeing. This examination illuminates proof based protection systems and adds to a more profound comprehension of the complex environmental elements at play.

4. **Backing and Strategy Impact:**
NGOs advocate for tiger protection at neighborhood, public, and global levels. Through strategy investigation, public mindfulness crusades, and direct commitment with chiefs, NGOs endeavor to impact regulation and arrangements that influence tiger natural surroundings and insurance. Their support endeavors are essential in establishing an empowering climate for powerful preservation activities.

5. **Limit Building:**

Numerous NGOs take part in limit building drives, giving preparation and backing to neighborhood networks, administrative offices, and different partners. By upgrading the abilities and information on those engaged with preservation, NGOs add to the supportability and long haul effect of drives.

III. Legislative Associations in Tiger Preservation

1. **Strategy Detailing and Execution:**
Legislative associations, including untamed life divisions and natural organizations, assume a focal part in the plan and execution of strategies connected with tiger protection. These associations foster legitimate structures, safeguarded region assignments, and guidelines that administer untamed life assurance and territory conservation. Their position is instrumental in making an establishment for fruitful protection endeavors.

2. **Authorization and Against Poaching Measures:**
Administrative associations are liable for authorizing untamed life assurance regulations and executing hostile to poaching measures. This includes the sending of woodland gatekeepers, watches, and the coordination of policing to battle criminal operations like poaching and dealing. Reinforcing these endeavors is significant in checking the dangers presented to Sumatran tigers.

3. **Worldwide Joint effort:**
As caretakers of public interests, legislative associations take part in worldwide coordinated efforts to address cross-line preservation challenges. Organizations with adjoining nations, worldwide bodies, and arrangements, for example, the Show on Global Exchange Imperiled Types of Wild Fauna and Greenery (Refers

to) work with composed endeavors to battle untamed life dealing and safeguard tiger populaces.

4. **Examination and Checking:**
   Administrative associations dispense assets for logical exploration and checking programs. These drives give basic information to confirm based navigation, empowering legislatures to evaluate the viability of protection methodologies, track populace drifts, and adjust approaches depending on the situation.

5. **Local area Commitment and Schooling:**

Perceiving the significance of local area contribution, administrative associations carry out programs that draw in neighborhood occupants in protection exercises. Schooling efforts, studios, and effort drives plan to bring issues to light about the worth of natural life, the significance of biodiversity, and the job people can play in protection endeavors.

IV. Difficulties and Cooperative energies in Cooperative Protection

1. **Correspondence and Coordination Difficulties:**
   Notwithstanding the common objective of tiger protection, correspondence and coordination difficulties can emerge among neighborhood networks, NGOs, and administrative associations. Contrasts in needs, approaches, and correspondence styles might thwart powerful cooperation. Laying out clear channels of correspondence, cultivating trust, and guaranteeing that all partners have a voice in navigation are fundamental for defeating these difficulties.

2. **Restricted Assets and Subsidizing Holes:**
   Both nearby networks and NGOs frequently face asset limitations. Nearby people group might miss the mark on monetary means to carry out supportable practices, while NGOs might battle to get long haul subsidizing for their protection projects. Connecting these asset holes requires imaginative subsidizing models, public-private organizations, and a guarantee to maintainable funding.

3. **Strategy and Lawful Difficulties:**
   At times, strategy and legitimate structures may not line up with the targets of preservation drives. Obsolete or clashing regulations, regulatory obstacles, and inadequate requirement can obstruct progress.
   Backing endeavors by NGOs and coordinated effort with legislative associations are critical for tending to these difficulties and establishing an empowering legitimate climate for preservation.

4. **Adjusting Protection and Improvement:**

The strain between protection needs and improvement plans represents a never-ending challenge. Legislative associations might confront strain to focus on monetary advancement over protection, prompting living space annihilation and expanded human-untamed life struggle. Finding some kind of harmony that obliges both protection and maintainable improvement is a complex yet essential endeavor.

V. The Way Forward: Fortifying Cooperative Protection

1. **Improving People group Inclusion:**
   Perceiving the one of a kind job of nearby networks as caretakers of their environments, preservation drives ought to endeavor to upgrade local area inclusion. This includes cultivating participatory independent direction, regarding neighborhood information, and fitting preservation procedures to line up with the requirements and yearnings of these networks.

2. **Advancing Cooperative Administration:**
   Legislative associations, NGOs, and neighborhood networks ought to pursue laying out cooperative administration structures. By encouraging associations, advancing straightforwardness, and integrating assorted points of view into dynamic cycles, these elements can aggregately address difficulties and drive compelling preservation results.

3. **Putting resources into Training and Mindfulness:**
   An educated and drew openly is urgent for the outcome of protection drives. Administrative associations and NGOs ought to keep on putting resources into training and mindfulness programs that feature the significance of biodiversity, the worth of tigers in environments, and the job people and networks play in preservation.

4. **Creative Subsidizing Models:**
   Tending to financing holes requires inventive methodologies. Legislatures can investigate public-private organizations, NGOs can broaden their money sources, and neighborhood networks can be upheld in creating feasible pay producing exercises that add to both preservation and local area prosperity.

5. **Versatile Administration and Exploration:**

Preservation endeavors ought to embrace versatile administration moves toward that consolidate progressing research discoveries. Customary observing, evaluation of results, and an eagerness to change procedures in view of new data are fundamental for guaranteeing the versatility and viability of protection drives.

Chapter 6

Challenges And Solutions

The preservation of Sumatran tigers presents a diverse and complex test, formed by a bunch of interconnected factors. As endeavors are embraced to safeguard these imperiled large felines, an extensive comprehension of the difficulties confronted is fundamental. This broad investigation digs into the different scope of difficulties defying Sumatran tiger protection, offering experiences into potential arrangements that can direct the way forward.

1. **Natural surroundings Misfortune and Fracture**
1. **Challenge:**
   Natural surroundings misfortune and fracture address one of the main dangers to Sumatran tigers. The quick extension of agribusiness, logging, and foundation improvement has prompted the contracting and fracture of their regular territories. This restricts the accessible space for tigers as well as upsets natural availability, adding to hereditary detachment and diminished biodiversity.
2. **Arrangement:**

Tending to living space misfortune requires a multi-pronged methodology. State run administrations and preservation associations can attempt to assign and safeguard basic tiger natural surroundings as public stops or saves. Moreover, advancing economical land-use rehearses, reforestation drives, and coordinating preservation contemplations into local advancement plans can assist with relieving the effect of living space misfortune.

II. Human-Natural life Struggle

1. **Challenge:**
   Human-natural life struggle emerges when tigers infringe upon human settlements, going after domesticated animals and setting off retaliatory activities from nearby networks. This contention not just represents an immediate danger

to individual tigers yet additionally adds to negative impression of these creatures, putting forth preservation attempts testing.

2. **Arrangement:**

Executing viable measures to alleviate human-natural life struggle is significant. This incorporates the improvement of early advance notice frameworks, secure lodging for animals, and local area based drives that give pay to misfortunes.

Instruction programs pointed toward bringing issues to light about tiger conduct, advancing conjunction, and displaying the financial advantages of living close by tigers can cultivate uplifting outlooks inside networks.

III. Unlawful Poaching and Natural life Dealing

1. **Challenge:**
The unlawful poaching of Sumatran tigers for their body parts, driven by request in conventional Asian medication and the extravagance market, stays a tenacious danger. Notwithstanding global endeavors to battle untamed life dealing, coordinated criminal organizations keep on taking advantage of these superb animals for benefit.

2. **Arrangement:**

Combatting unlawful poaching requires improved enemy of poaching measures, stricter policing, global coordinated effort. Hostile to poaching units outfitted with current innovation, for example, camera traps and robots, can further develop reconnaissance in weak regions. Reinforcing regulation, forcing extreme punishments for untamed life violations, and disturbing dealing networks through global collaboration are necessary parts of an exhaustive arrangement.

IV. Absence of Subsidizing and Assets

1. **Challenge:**
Restricted subsidizing represents a critical obstacle to the viable execution of preservation drives. The expenses related with living space assurance, against poaching measures, exploration, and local area commitment frequently surpass accessible assets.

2. **Arrangement:**

Creative subsidizing models and expanded cooperation are basic to address the monetary requirements of protection. Legislatures can distribute more assets to untamed life security, and NGOs can investigate public-private associations, charitable drives, and crowdfunding. Drawing in neighborhood networks in maintainable pay creating exercises can add to both protection and monetary turn of events.

V. Environmental Change Effect

1. **Challenge:**
   The speeding up effects of environmental change represent extra dangers to Sumatran tigers and their living spaces. Changes in temperature, precipitation designs, and the recurrence of outrageous climate occasions can disturb environments, adjust prey accessibility, and fuel existing preservation challenges.
2. **Arrangement:**

Coordinating environmental change versatility into preservation arranging is fundamental. This includes recognizing and carrying out procedures to assist the two tigers and their living spaces with adjusting to changing natural circumstances. Also, upholding for worldwide endeavors to relieve environmental change can add to the drawn out suitability of tiger territories.

VI. Political Will and Administration

1. **Challenge:**
   The progress of protection endeavors is in many cases dependent upon political will and viable administration. In certain areas, frail requirement of ecological regulations, defilement, and clashing advancement plans keep on sabotaging protection drives.
2. **Arrangement:**

Promotion and mindfulness missions can be instrumental in collecting political help for tiger protection. Reinforcing natural administration, further developing policing, drawing in with policymakers to coordinate preservation needs into advancement plans are fundamental stages. Worldwide strain and cooperation can likewise impact legislatures to focus on protection endeavors.

VII. Lacking Exploration and Observing

1. **Challenge:**
   Restricted comprehension of the biology, conduct, and strength of Sumatran tigers upsets the advancement of compelling preservation procedures. Insufficient examination and checking can prompt an absence of information driven navigation and a diminished ability to survey the effect of protection mediations.
2. **Arrangement:**

Putting resources into exhaustive exploration programs is basic for tending to information holes. Using trend setting innovations, for example, camera traps, satellite following, and hereditary examination can give important experiences. Long haul observing drives can follow populace patterns, evaluate the outcome of protection intercessions, and illuminate versatile administration draws near.

VIII. Adjusting Protection and Advancement

1. **Challenge:**
   The strain between preservation needs and financial improvement represents a test. Tensions to take advantage of normal assets for financial addition can prompt natural surroundings annihilation, further undermining the endurance of Sumatran tigers.
2. **Arrangement:**

Finding some kind of harmony among protection and improvement requires a comprehensive methodology. Executing manageable advancement works on, advancing eco-accommodating businesses, and integrating protection contemplations into land-use arranging are fundamental. Coordinated effort between protectionists, policymakers, and organizations can encourage a commonly helpful relationship that upholds both monetary development and natural life preservation.

IX. Public Mindfulness and Training

1. **Challenge:**
   Lacking public mindfulness about the significance of Sumatran tigers, the dangers they face, and the job people can play in preservation obstructs aggregate endeavors to safeguard these lofty creatures.
2. **Arrangement:**

Instructive projects and public mindfulness crusades are instrumental in tending to this test. These drives ought to zero in on schools, nearby networks, and the more extensive public, underlining the worth of biodiversity, the meaning of Sumatran tigers in keeping up with biological system balance, and the common obligation regarding their preservation. Drawing in the media and utilizing social stages can enhance the scope of protection messages.

X. Financial Variables and Neediness

1. **Challenge:**
   In areas where neediness is predominant, neighborhood networks might depend on exercises that adversely influence tiger natural surroundings, like logging or unlawful hunting, for monetary endurance.
2. **Arrangement:**

Tending to the underlying drivers of these exercises requires a two dimensional methodology. Preservation drives can offer elective work open doors, for example, eco-the travel industry or feasible horticulture, to decrease reliance on destructive practices. All the while, destitution mitigation programs that attention on training and expertise advancement can engage networks to pursue ecologically cognizant decisions.

Toward Supportable Arrangements

The difficulties looked in the preservation of Sumatran tigers are mind boggling and interconnected, requiring an all encompassing and cooperative methodology. While the street ahead is trying, there are reasonable arrangements that can direct preservation endeavors toward progress. By tending to natural surroundings misfortune, relieving human-untamed life struggle, combatting unlawful poaching, getting sufficient financing, adjusting to environmental change, and encouraging political will, partners can add to the drawn out endurance of Sumatran tigers. The collaboration between neighborhood networks, NGOs, legislative associations, and the more extensive public is fundamental for exploring these difficulties and guaranteeing a future where Sumatran tigers keep on meandering the woods of Sumatra. As we face these difficulties head-on, the obligation to preservation should stay resolute, driven by the comprehension that the destiny of the Sumatran tiger is indistinguishable from the wellbeing and strength of our common planet.

6.1Identification and analysis of the challenges faced by conservationists in safeguarding Sumatran tigers.

The protection of Sumatran tigers, Panthera tigris sumatrae, is a complicated and testing try that requires a nuanced comprehension of the different snags looked by progressives. As these glorious large felines explore the dangers presented by environment misfortune, human-natural life struggle, unlawful poaching, and other interconnected issues, preservation endeavors should develop to successfully address these difficulties. This top to bottom examination dives into the ID and examination of the diverse difficulties looked by preservationists in shielding Sumatran tigers, investigating the complexities of every impediment and proposing possible answers for a manageable concurrence among people and these imperiled cats.

1. **Natural surroundings Misfortune and Fracture**
1. **Recognizable proof:**
   Natural surroundings misfortune and fracture are among the most basic difficulties looked by moderates attempting to safeguard Sumatran tigers. The extensive and various scenes that these large felines once wandered are progressively being changed into agrarian regions, logging concessions, and foundation projects. This deficiency of territory lessens the accessible space for tigers as well as sections their populaces, prompting hereditary disconnection and an expanded gamble of inbreeding.

2. **Investigation:**
The investigation of living space misfortune and fracture uncovers a mind boggling interchange of financial turn of events, populace development, and contending land-use interests.

Fast deforestation driven by palm oil manors and logging exercises essentially lessens the tiger's regular reach. Fracture worsens the difficulties by segregating tiger populaces, making it hard for people to track down mates and keep up with hereditary variety. The results of these cycles stretch out past the quick dangers, influencing the drawn out suitability of Sumatran tiger populaces.

3. **Expected Arrangements:**

Protectionists should work cooperatively with state run administrations, nearby networks, and organizations to address territory misfortune and discontinuity. Carrying out and fortifying safeguarded regions, public parks, and natural life passageways is vital. Supporting for economical land-use rehearses, reforestation drives, and integrating protection contemplations into improvement plans are fundamental parts of the arrangement. Long haul achievement requires a comprehensive methodology that adjusts the necessities of the two people and tigers.

II. Human-Natural life Struggle

1. **Distinguishing proof:**
Human-natural life struggle emerges when tigers clash with neighborhood networks, frequently because of predation on domesticated animals. This contention represents a huge danger to the two tigers and the networks they influence. Retaliatory killings, dread, and negative view of tigers can prompt further danger of these enormous felines.

2. **Investigation:**
The investigation of human-natural life struggle highlights the difficulties presented by the vicinity of tiger living spaces to human settlements. As human populaces venture into customary tiger domains, the probability of collaborations and clashes increments. Animals misfortunes bring about financial difficulties for nearby networks, prompting negative impression of tigers as dangers to occupations. This dynamic makes a pattern of contention that is negative to both human networks and tiger populaces.

3. **Expected Arrangements:**

Tending to human-untamed life struggle requires a blend of proactive measures and local area commitment. Preservationists can work with neighborhood networks to execute secure animals lodging, early admonition frameworks, and remuneration programs for domesticated animals misfortunes. Training drives that advance concurrence, bring issues to light about tiger conduct, and feature the biological significance of these hunters can cultivate uplifting perspectives. Long haul arrangements include creating economical business options that lessen reliance on exercises clashing with tiger protection objectives.

III. Unlawful Poaching and Natural life Dealing

1. **Distinguishing proof:**
   Unlawful poaching for the unlawful natural life exchange stays a relentless and extreme test for Sumatran tiger preservation. Interest for tiger parts, driven by conventional Asian medication and the extravagance market, powers a rewarding unlawful exchange organization. Notwithstanding global endeavors to battle natural life dealing, the poaching of Sumatran tigers proceeds.

2. **Examination:**
   The examination of unlawful poaching uncovers a complicated snare of coordinated wrongdoing organizations, defilement, and lacking implementation of natural life security regulations. The interest for tiger parts, frequently filled by social convictions and strange notions, adds to the determined quest for these jeopardized creatures. Powerless legitimate structures, permeable boundaries, and the high benefit of the unlawful untamed life exchange present imposing difficulties to traditionalists attempting to control poaching exercises.

3. **Possible Arrangements:**

Protectionists should team up with legislatures, policing, and global associations to actually battle unlawful poaching. Reinforcing against poaching measures, conveying cutting edge innovations, for example, camera traps and robots, and expanding punishments for natural life wrongdoings are basic advances. Global collaboration to destroy dealing organizations, bring issues to light about the results of the unlawful untamed life exchange, and address the interest for tiger parts is fundamental for long haul achievement.

IV. Absence of Financing and Assets

1. **Recognizable proof:**
   Restricted financing represents a huge hindrance to preservation endeavors pointed toward protecting Sumatran tigers. The expenses related with living space assurance, hostile to poaching measures, exploration, and local area commitment frequently surpass accessible assets, blocking the execution and manageability of preservation drives.

2. **Investigation:**
   The investigation of subsidizing difficulties uncovers an inconsistency between the size of protection needs and the accessible monetary assets. Preservation projects frequently go after restricted subsidizing, and the drawn out nature of tiger protection needs supported monetary help.

Also, monetary limitations looked by neighborhood networks might ruin their dynamic cooperation in preservation endeavors, further fueling the test.

3. **Expected Arrangements:**

Imaginative subsidizing models are vital for address the monetary imperatives looked by protectionists. State run administrations can allot more assets to untamed life security, and NGOs can broaden their sources of financial support through open confidential associations, corporate sponsorships, and humanitarian drives. Drawing in the confidential area in economical strategic policies that add to preservation objectives can likewise make new roads for financing.

V. Environmental Change Effect

1. **Distinguishing proof:**
   The effects of environmental change present an extra layer of intricacy for Sumatran tiger protection. Changes in temperature, precipitation designs, and the recurrence of outrageous climate occasions can disturb biological systems, adjust prey accessibility, and fuel existing difficulties looked by these jeopardized huge felines.

2. **Investigation:**
   The investigation of environmental change influences on Sumatran tigers features the weakness of these species to natural changes. Changed vegetation designs, changes in prey dissemination, and expanded recurrence of outrageous climate occasions present direct dangers to tiger natural surroundings and food sources. Also, environmental change-instigated living space debasement can intensify existing difficulties, making it more moving for tiger populaces to adjust and get by.

3. **Likely Arrangements:**

Preservationists should incorporate environmental change versatility into their systems. This includes distinguishing and executing versatile administration estimates that assist the two tigers and their living spaces with adapting to changing ecological circumstances. Cooperative endeavors to moderate environmental change on a worldwide scale are fundamental, as the effects on Sumatran tigers are not restricted to nearby or public limits.

VI. Political Will and Administration

1. **ID:**
   The progress of preservation endeavors is intently attached to political will and successful administration. In certain areas, powerless implementation of natural regulations, debasement, and clashing improvement plans keep on sabotaging protection drives.

2. **Examination:**

The examination of political will and administration challenges uncovers a perplexing scene where preservation objectives might struggle with transient monetary interests. The abuse of regular assets for financial advancement can overshadow the security of tiger territories. Inadequate requirement of ecological regulations, defilement inside legislative organizations, and an absence of combination of preservation needs into more extensive improvement plans add to the obstacles looked by moderates.

3. **Expected Arrangements:**

Promotion endeavors are critical to accumulate political help for tiger preservation. Moderates can attempt to bring issues to light about the natural significance of Sumatran tigers, drawing in with policymakers to focus on protection inside public plans. Reinforcing ecological administration, further developing policing, working together with legislative organizations are fundamental stages toward cultivating political will and compelling administration.

VII. Insufficient Exploration and Observing

1. **Distinguishing proof:**

Insufficient examination and checking frustrate the improvement of compelling protection systems for Sumatran tigers. The absence of thorough information on the environment, conduct, and soundness of these enormous felines restricts the ability to pursue informed choices and evaluate the effect of protection intercessions.

2. **Examination:**

The examination of exploration and checking difficulties highlights the requirement for a more profound comprehension of Sumatran tiger populaces. Restricted assets and specialized difficulties might block the execution of far reaching research programs. The shortfall of powerful checking drives can bring about an absence of information driven navigation, frustrating versatile administration approaches fundamental for the outcome of preservation endeavors.

3. **Expected Arrangements:**

Putting resources into research drives that use cutting edge innovations, for example, camera traps, satellite following, and hereditary examination, is fundamental. Cooperation with research foundations, worldwide associations, and neighborhood networks can upgrade the assortment of significant information. Long haul observing projects that track populace patterns, evaluate the outcome of preservation intercessions, and illuminate versatile administration are basic for the manageability of protection drives.

VIII. Adjusting Preservation and Advancement

1. **ID:**
   Finding some kind of harmony between preservation needs and financial improvement is a tireless test. Tensions to take advantage of regular assets for financial increase can prompt environment annihilation, further undermining the endurance of Sumatran tigers.

2. **Investigation:**
   The investigation of the protection and improvement challenge uncovers a fragile equilibrium that should be accomplished to guarantee the concurrence of people and tigers. Clashing needs, particularly in areas where financial improvement is focused on over preservation, can bring about unreasonable land-use practices, deforestation, and expanded human-natural life struggle.

3. **Expected Arrangements:**

The arrangement lies in carrying out manageable improvement rehearses that focus on preservation close by monetary development. Protectionists can team up with organizations to advance eco-accommodating businesses, participate in mindful the travel industry rehearses, and coordinate preservation contemplations into land-use arranging. Finding some kind of harmony that obliges both protection and reasonable improvement requires coordinated effort between progressives, policymakers, and organizations.

IX. Public Mindfulness and Instruction

1. **ID:**
   Lacking public mindfulness about the significance of Sumatran tigers, the dangers they face, and the job people can play in preservation hinders aggregate endeavors to safeguard these radiant creatures.

2. **Examination:**
   The examination of public mindfulness challenges uncovers a hole in information and comprehension of the biological meaning of Sumatran tigers. Public discernments might be impacted by social convictions, and an absence of mindfulness can add to detachment or even resistance to preservation drives. Media portrayal and instructive effort assume pivotal parts in molding public mentalities toward tiger protection.

3. **Expected Arrangements:**

Instructive projects and public mindfulness crusades are instrumental in tending to this test. Protectionists can team up with news sources, schools, and nearby networks to disperse precise data about Sumatran tigers.

Drawing in with social stages, utilizing narrating, and making convincing accounts that feature the interconnectedness of people and tigers can enhance the compass of protection messages.

X. Financial Variables and Destitution

1. Recognizable proof:

Financial elements, including destitution, can drive networks to participate in exercises destructive to Sumatran tigers, like logging or unlawful hunting.

2. Examination:

The examination of financial difficulties uncovers a mind boggling dynamic where destitution and restricted monetary open doors might prompt the double-dealing of regular assets for endurance. Neighborhood people group confronting monetary difficulties might turn to exercises that adversely influence tiger territories, adding to living space misfortune, and expanded human-natural life struggle.

3. Possible Arrangements:

Tending to the underlying drivers of these exercises requires a far reaching approach. Preservation drives can offer elective job valuable open doors that are both financially suitable and earth reasonable. Neediness easing programs that emphasis on training and expertise improvement can engage networks to go with naturally cognizant decisions, adding to both financial prosperity and tiger protection.

6.2 Exploration of innovative solutions and strategies to overcome these challenges.

As the protection of Sumatran tigers faces a large number of difficulties, the quest for imaginative arrangements and procedures becomes basic. The intricacies of environment misfortune, human-natural life struggle, unlawful poaching, and other interconnected issues request innovative methodologies that address the underlying drivers and advance long haul manageability. In this investigation, we dive into creative arrangements and methodologies that can enable traditionalists to beat the difficulties looked in protecting Sumatran tigers.

1. Feasible Innovation for Against Poaching Endeavors

1. Advancement:

Utilizing practical innovation, for example, high level camera traps, robots, and sensor organizations, can reform against poaching endeavors. These apparatuses give continuous observing of tiger living spaces, recognize criminal operations, and empower fast reaction components.

2. Benefits:

Maintainable innovation improves the productivity and inclusion of against poaching drives. Camera traps offer non-meddlesome checking, while robots can watch tremendous regions rapidly. Sensor networks give nonstop information, empowering convenient intercessions and decreasing the dependence on labor supply escalated watches.

3. Execution:

Protection associations and administrative organizations can team up with innovation organizations to execute and adjust these apparatuses to the particular necessities of Sumatran tiger preservation. Preparing neighborhood groups in the utilization of these advancements guarantees supported viability.

II. Feasible Supporting Models

1. **Advancement:**
   Creating feasible supporting models that mix protection with monetary interests can make a self-supporting environment. Drives like installment for biological system administrations (PES), eco-the travel industry, and carbon credits can produce assets while cultivating natural stewardship.

2. **Benefits:**
   Economical funding models give a solid income stream to protection endeavors. By adjusting financial motivations to protection objectives, these models make a commonly building up connection between monetary turn of events and ecological conservation.

3. **Execution:**

States, NGOs, and nearby networks can team up to lay out and advance feasible funding models. Carrying out eco-the travel industry drives that feature the magnificence of Sumatran tigers and their territories can draw in guests, creating income while bringing issues to light about the significance of preservation.

III. Local area Based Protection and Business Advancement

1. **Advancement:**
   Coordinating people group based preservation drives with manageable job advancement projects can address human-untamed life struggle. This includes turning out elective revenue amazing open doors for neighborhood networks that diminish dependence on exercises negative to tiger natural surroundings.

2. **Benefits:**
   Engaging nearby networks to become dynamic stewards of their current circumstance encourages a feeling of pride and obligation. By offering suitable options in contrast to rehearses that hurt tiger living spaces, local area based protection drives add to long haul conjunction.

3. **Execution:**

Protectionists can team up with neighborhood networks to distinguish and carry out feasible job programs. This could remember preparing for eco-accommodating agribusiness, supporting local area oversaw saves, or laying out cooperatives for reasonable asset usage.

IV. Environment Versatile Protection Techniques

1. **Development:**

    Creating environment versatile protection techniques includes incorporating environmental change variation measures into Sumatran tiger preservation arranging. This incorporates understanding and tending to the effects of environmental change on tiger territories and prey accessibility.

2. **Benefits:**

    Environment versatile techniques guarantee that preservation endeavors stay viable notwithstanding changing ecological circumstances. By proactively tending to the effects of environmental change, traditionalists can upgrade the drawn out suitability of Sumatran tiger populaces.

3. **Execution:**

Preservation associations, analysts, and administrative organizations can team up to evaluate the weakness of tiger living spaces to environmental change. This data can then illuminate versatile administration procedures, guaranteeing that protection endeavors stay viable even with an evolving environment.

V. Public-Private Organizations for Natural surroundings Assurance

1. **Advancement:**

    Shaping public-private associations (PPPs) for environment security includes joint effort between government bodies, confidential ventures, and protection associations. This model can use the assets and ability, everything being equal, to make extensive preservation plans.

2. **Benefits:**

    PPPs work with the pooling of monetary assets, specialized skill, and neighborhood information. This cooperative methodology can prompt more powerful natural surroundings insurance, further developed implementation, and a more all encompassing protection procedure.

3. **Execution:**

States can make systems that urge private undertakings to put resources into preservation. This could include charge motivators, administrative help, or direct associations. Preservation associations can go about as mediators, working with coordinated effort and guaranteeing that the interests of both the confidential area and protection are adjusted.

VI. Instruction and Mindfulness through Innovation

1. **Development:**
Using innovation, like computer generated simulation (VR) and increased reality (AR), for instruction and mindfulness missions can draw in a more extensive crowd. VR and AR encounters can move people into the universe of Sumatran tigers, cultivating a more profound association and understanding.

2. **Benefits:**
Innovation driven instructive drives can contact worldwide crowds, bringing issues to light about the difficulties looked by Sumatran tigers and the significance of their protection. This approach can possibly produce public help and support economical practices.

3. **Execution:**

Preservation associations can team up with innovation engineers, content makers, and instructive foundations to plan vivid encounters. These can be dispersed through web-based stages, instructive organizations, and public mindfulness occasions, guaranteeing an extensive range.

VII. Versatile Co-Administration of Preservation Regions

1. **Development:**
Carrying out versatile co-administration includes encouraging cooperative dynamic cycles that incorporate neighborhood networks, legislative offices, and moderates. This approach considers adaptability in protection methodologies in view of developing circumstances.

2. **Benefits:**
Versatile co-administration perceives the unique idea of environments and the requirement for adaptable preservation systems. By including nearby networks in direction, it advances a feeling of shared liability and guarantees that preservation endeavors line up with neighborhood necessities and goals.

3. **Execution:**

Progressives can start cooperative stages where all partners partake in navigation. Normal appraisals and criticism circles guarantee that preservation procedures stay pertinent and versatile to evolving conditions.

VIII. Multi-Partner Stages for Strategy Promotion

1. **Development:**
Laying out multi-partner stages for strategy support includes uniting assorted substances, including preservation associations, government agents, organizations, and neighborhood networks. These stages advocate for arrangements that focus on Sumatran tiger protection.

2. **Benefits:**
   Multi-partner stages enhance the aggregate voice for protection, affecting strategy choices at different levels. By cultivating exchange and joint effort, these stages can connect holes in understanding and adjust assorted interests toward normal preservation objectives.
3. **Execution:**

Preservation associations can start to lead the pack in framing and working with multi-partner stages. These stages ought to zero in on building agreement, supporting for strategy changes, and cultivating cooperative drives that benefit the two tigers and the networks sharing their territories.

Chapter 7

Success Stories

Sumatran tiger protection has seen the two difficulties and victories, with committed endeavors from different partners. This investigation of examples of overcoming adversity means to reveal insight into rousing accomplishments, creative methodologies, and the significant illustrations learned in the continuous fight to protect this jeopardized species.

1. The Progress of Kerinci Seblat Public Park

Kerinci Seblat Public Park, situated on the island of Sumatra, stands apart as an example of overcoming adversity in Sumatran tiger protection. Laid out in 1982, this park is quite possibly of the biggest safeguarded region in Indonesia and gives basic living space to the Sumatran tiger. The outcome of Kerinci Seblat can be credited to:

1. **Powerful Safeguarded Region The board:**
   The recreation area's administration has executed strong enemy of poaching measures, including expanded officer watches, the utilization of current reconnaissance innovation, and local area commitment. This has essentially diminished criminal operations inside the recreation area.
2. **Local area Contribution:**
   Neighborhood people group encompassing Kerinci Seblat have been effectively engaged with protection endeavors. Practical job projects, for example, eco-the travel industry drives and local area based backwoods the executives, have decreased human-natural life struggle as well as cultivated a feeling of shared liability regarding tiger preservation.
3. **Exploration and Observing:**

The recreation area's administration has focused on exploration and observing projects, using trend setting innovations, for example, camera traps and satellite following. This information driven approach has given significant bits of knowledge into tiger conduct, populace elements, and territory utilization, empowering informed independent direction.

II. Imaginative Protection Models in Harapan Rainforest

The Harapan Rainforest Protection Task, started in 2007, is a novel and imaginative model that joins preservation with reasonable turn of events. Situated in the Jambi and South Sumatra areas, this venture has shown accomplishment through:

1. **Monetary Practicality through Supportable Logging:**
   Harapan Rainforest consolidates maintainable logging works on, producing income while safeguarding the uprightness of the biological system. This approach guarantees that monetary improvement lines up with preservation objectives, finding some kind of harmony between human requirements and tiger territory security.

2. **Local area Strengthening:**
   The task underscores the significance of local area contribution in protection. Nearby people group are furnished with preparing in practical farming, non-wood backwoods item gathering, and eco-the travel industry, making elective occupations that lessen reliance on exercises unsafe to tiger territories.

3. **Territory Rebuilding and Biodiversity Preservation:**

Harapan Rainforest incorporates dynamic territory rebuilding drives, zeroing in on reforestation and the restoration of debased regions. The rebuilding endeavors contribute not exclusively to tiger protection yet additionally to the general biodiversity of the district.

III. Protection through Cooperation: The Worldwide Tiger Drive

On a worldwide scale, the Worldwide Tiger Drive (GTI), sent off in 2010, addresses a cooperative exertion including different nations, associations, and partners. This drive intends to twofold the quantity of wild tigers by 2022 and has made striking progress through:

1. **Global Participation:**
   The GTI cultivates joint effort between tiger-range nations, global associations, and traditionalists. This aggregate methodology addresses transboundary issues, for example, unlawful untamed life exchange and territory network, perceiving that the protection of Sumatran tigers requires a worldwide exertion.

2. **Interest in Enemy of Poaching Measures:**
   Part nations of the GTI have put altogether in enemy of poaching measures, including the reinforcing of policing, of innovation for observation, and limit working for officers. This has prompted a decrease in poaching occurrences and an expansion in tiger populaces in certain locales.

3. **Public Mindfulness and Backing:**

The GTI puts major areas of strength for an on open mindfulness and backing to gather support for tiger preservation. Crusades, instructive projects, and media commitment have helped bring issues to light about the situation of tigers, producing public help for preservation drives.

IV. Movement Achievement: The Instance of Bukit Barisan Selatan Public Park

Bukit Barisan Selatan Public Park in Sumatra has encountered accomplishment through a movement program pointed toward expanding the dispersion and hereditary variety of Sumatran tigers. Key elements adding to this achievement include:

1. **Hereditary Variety Improvement:**
   Movement endeavors included migrating tigers from regions with higher populaces to districts where hereditary variety was low. This procedure planned to moderate the gamble of inbreeding, improving the general wellbeing and flexibility of the tiger populace.

2. **Natural surroundings Assurance and Reclamation:**
   The progress of movement was supplemented by simultaneous endeavors to safeguard and reestablish tiger natural surroundings inside Bukit Barisan Selatan Public Park. Hostile to poaching measures and local area commitment drives added to establishing a favorable climate for the moved tigers.

3. **Observing and Versatile Administration:**

Thorough observing, including the utilization of satellite following, permitted moderates to survey the progress of movements and adjust methodologies in view of the way of behaving and prosperity of the moved tigers. This versatile administration approach has been critical in guaranteeing the supported progress of the program.

V. Local area Oversaw Stores in Kerinci

Kerinci, a locale known for its importance in Sumatran tiger protection, has seen a good outcome through the foundation of local area oversaw saves. Key components adding to this achievement include:

1. **Neighborhood Strengthening and Proprietorship:**
   Networks in Kerinci effectively partake in the administration of nearby holds, encouraging a feeling of pride and obligation. This commitment guarantees that protection systems line up with the necessities and yearnings of neighborhood occupants.

2. **Feasible Farming Practices:**
   The execution of feasible farming practices inside local area oversaw holds diminishes the strain on tiger natural surroundings. Agroforestry models and

natural cultivating methods are utilized, advancing biodiversity while giving monetary advantages to nearby networks.

3. **The travel industry as a Preservation Device:**

Local area oversaw saves in Kerinci influence eco-the travel industry as a protection device. This creates income for nearby networks as well as brings issues to light among guests about the significance of safeguarding Sumatran tigers and their environments.

VI. Preservation Training Drives: The Job of Zoos

Zoos and natural life preservation focuses play had a huge impact in Sumatran tiger protection through schooling drives. Fruitful models include:

1. **Ex Situ Preservation and Reproducing Projects:**
   Zoos take part in ex situ preservation endeavors, keeping up with hereditarily different hostage populaces of Sumatran tigers. Reproducing programs add to the general preservation objectives by guaranteeing a repository of hereditary variety.

2. **Public Commitment and Instruction:**
   Zoos effectively connect with the general population in protection through instructive projects, intelligent displays, and effort drives. These endeavors intend to bring issues to light about the difficulties looked by Sumatran tigers and the significance of worldwide protection.

3. **Support for In Situ Preservation:**

Numerous zoos allot assets and financing to help in situ preservation projects in the regular territories of Sumatran tigers. This cooperative methodology guarantees an all encompassing technique that consolidates ex situ and in situ preservation endeavors.

VII. Outcome in Restoration and Delivery Projects

Recovery and delivery programs have shown outcome in reestablishing Sumatran tigers to their regular natural surroundings. Key components adding to progress include:

1. **Salvage and Restoration:**
   Programs that salvage and restore harmed or stranded Sumatran tigers assume a vital part in their preservation. Veterinary consideration, recovery offices, and conduct preparing add to planning people for discharge.

2. **Discharge into Safeguarded Regions:**
   Fruitful projects include delivering restored tigers into all around safeguarded and reasonable environments. This guarantees that delivered people get an opportunity to flourish, adding to the wild populace.

3. **Post-Delivery Observing:**

Thorough post-discharge checking, including satellite following and on-the-ground perceptions, is fundamental to evaluate the progress of recovery and delivery programs. Versatile administration in view of observing information adds to the refinement of delivery methodologies.

VIII. Native Information Joining in Preservation

In some effective preservation drives, the reconciliation of native information and practices has demonstrated gainful. Native people group have illustrated:

1. **Conventional Environmental Information:**
   Native people group frequently have important conventional environmental information about nearby biological systems, including the way of behaving of untamed life like Sumatran tigers. Coordinating this information into protection techniques upgrades the viability of preservation endeavors.

2. **Local area drove Protection Practices:**
   Cooperative endeavors that regard and include native networks in protection navigation engage them to go about as caretakers of their normal environmental elements. This can prompt more economical and socially delicate preservation rehearses.

3. **Adjusting Protection and Social Legacy:**

Perceiving the harmonious connection between native societies and the climate, effective drives work out some kind of harmony between protection objectives and the safeguarding of social legacy. This approach cultivates an amicable concurrence among people and Sumatran tigers.

IX. The Job of Worldwide NGOs: Preservation Global's Progress in Tesso Nilo

Protection Worldwide's work in the Tesso Nilo scene represents the effect of global NGOs in Sumatran tiger preservation. Key components of accomplishment include:

1. **Limit Building and Neighborhood Associations:**
   Protection Global spotlights on building nearby limit and framing organizations with administrative offices and neighborhood networks. This approach guarantees that protection endeavors are educated by neighborhood information and needs.

2. **Backing for Strategy Change:**
   The association takes part in backing endeavors to impact strategy changes that favor Sumatran tiger preservation. By working with states and policymakers, Preservation Worldwide adds to the creation and requirement of regulations that safeguard tiger environments.

3. **Logical Exploration and Observing:**

Protection Worldwide underlines the significance of logical examination and checking in Tesso Nilo. This remembers reads up for tiger conduct, territory wellbeing, and the effects of human exercises. The information created illuminates protection methodologies and versatile administration.

7.1 Spotlight on successful case studies and examples of conservation efforts that have positively impacted Sumatran tiger populations.

The protection of Sumatran tigers, a jeopardized and notorious species, has been set apart by the two difficulties and triumphs. In this investigation, we focus on fruitful contextual analyses and instances of protection endeavors that decidedly affect Sumatran tiger populaces. These accounts offer bits of knowledge into compelling systems, inventive methodologies, and the cooperative endeavors of different partners, giving a diagram to future protection drives.

1. **Kerinci Seblat Public Park: A Shelter for Sumatran Tigers**
   Kerinci Seblat Public Park Outline:
   Laid out in 1982, Kerinci Seblat Public Park remains as perhaps of the biggest safeguarded region in Indonesia, enveloping different biological systems and filling in as basic environment for Sumatran tigers.
   Achievement Variables:
   Successful Enemy of Poaching Measures:
   Kerinci Seblat Public Park has carried out strong enemy of poaching measures, including expanded officer watches, the utilization of current reconnaissance innovation, and local area commitment. This extensive methodology has fundamentally decreased criminal operations inside the recreation area, giving a more secure climate to the tiger populace.
   Local area Inclusion and Maintainable Vocations:
   Nearby people group encompassing the recreation area effectively take part in protection endeavors. Supportable vocation projects, for example, eco-the travel industry drives and local area based woods the executives, have diminished human-natural life struggle as well as encouraged a feeling of shared liability regarding tiger preservation.
   Examination and Checking Drives:
   The recreation area's administration has focused on exploration and observing projects, using cutting edge innovations, for example, camera traps and satellite following. This information driven approach has given important experiences into tiger conduct, populace elements, and living space use, empowering informed navigation and versatile administration.

2. **Harapan Rainforest Protection Undertaking: Offsetting Preservation with Maintainable Turn of events**
   Harapan Rainforest Task Outline:
   Started in 2007, the Harapan Rainforest Protection Venture in Jambi and South

Sumatra regions addresses an imaginative model that consolidates preservation with manageable advancement rehearses.

Achievement Variables:

Reasonable Logging Practices:

The venture consolidates manageable logging works on, creating income while safeguarding the trustworthiness of the environment. By showing the way that monetary improvement can line up with preservation objectives, the venture finds some kind of harmony between human requirements and tiger living space security.

Local area Strengthening through Feasible Vocations:

Harapan Rainforest underscores the significance of local area contribution in preservation. Neighborhood people group are furnished with preparing in maintainable horticulture, non-wood backwoods item reaping, and eco-the travel industry, making elective occupations that decrease reliance on exercises hurtful to tiger environments.

Living space Reclamation Drives:

The undertaking incorporates dynamic living space rebuilding drives, zeroing in on reforestation and the restoration of debased regions. This obligation to environment rebuilding contributes not exclusively to tiger protection yet in addition to the general biodiversity of the area.

3. **Worldwide Tiger Drive: Cooperative Protection on a Worldwide Scale**

   Worldwide Tiger Drive (GTI) Outline:

   Sent off in 2010, the Worldwide Tiger Drive addresses a cooperative exertion including various nations, associations, and partners determined to twofold the quantity of wild tigers by 2022.

   Achievement Variables:

   Worldwide Participation:

   The GTI encourages cooperation between tiger-range nations, global associations, and progressives. This aggregate methodology addresses transboundary issues, for example, unlawful natural life exchange and living space network, perceiving that the preservation of Sumatran tigers requires a worldwide exertion.

   Interest in Enemy of Poaching Measures:

   Part nations of the GTI have put essentially in enemy of poaching measures, including the reinforcing of policing, of innovation for observation, and limit working for officers. This has prompted a decrease in poaching episodes and an expansion in tiger populaces in certain districts.

   Public Mindfulness and Backing:

   The GTI puts major areas of strength for an on open mindfulness and backing to earn support for tiger preservation. Crusades, instructive projects, and media commitment have helped bring issues to light about the predicament of tigers, creating public help for preservation drives.

4. **Movement Achievement: Upgrading Hereditary Variety in Bukit Barisan Selatan Public Park**

Bukit Barisan Selatan Public Park Outline:

Bukit Barisan Selatan Public Park in Sumatra has encountered accomplishment through a movement program pointed toward expanding the dissemination and hereditary variety of Sumatran tigers.

Achievement Variables:

Hereditary Variety Improvement:

Movement endeavors included migrating tigers from regions with higher populaces to districts where hereditary variety was low. This procedure planned to relieve the gamble of inbreeding, improving the general wellbeing and flexibility of the tiger populace.

Environment Security and Reclamation:

The progress of movement was supplemented by simultaneous endeavors to safeguard and reestablish tiger living spaces inside Bukit Barisan Selatan Public Park. Hostile to poaching measures and local area commitment drives added to establishing a helpful climate for the moved tigers.

Checking and Versatile Administration:

Thorough observing, including the utilization of satellite following, permitted traditionalists to survey the progress of movements and adjust techniques in view of the way of behaving and prosperity of the moved tigers. This versatile administration approach has been significant in guaranteeing the supported outcome of the program.

5. **Local area Oversaw Stores in Kerinci: Neighborhood Stewardship for Tiger Protection**

Kerinci People group Oversaw Stores Outline:

Kerinci, known for its importance in Sumatran tiger preservation, has seen a good outcome through the foundation of local area oversaw holds.

Achievement Variables:

Nearby Strengthening and Proprietorship:

Networks in Kerinci effectively take part in the administration of nearby saves, encouraging a feeling of pride and obligation. This commitment guarantees that protection systems line up with the necessities and yearnings of nearby inhabitants.

Supportable Farming Practices:

The execution of supportable farming practices inside local area oversaw holds diminishes the tension on tiger environments. Agroforestry models and natural cultivating procedures are utilized, advancing biodiversity while giving monetary advantages to nearby networks.

The travel industry as a Protection Device:

Local area oversaw holds in Kerinci influence eco-the travel industry as a preservation device. This produces income for nearby networks as well as brings issues to light among guests about the significance of safeguarding Sumatran tigers and their territories.

6. **Preservation Schooling Drives: Zoos and Natural life Protection Focuses**
   Zoo Preservation Drives Outline:

   Zoos and natural life preservation focuses play had a critical impact in Sumatran tiger protection through schooling drives and reproducing programs.

   Achievement Elements:

   Ex Situ Preservation and Rearing Projects:

   Zoos take part in ex situ protection endeavors, keeping up with hereditarily different hostage populaces of Sumatran tigers. Reproducing programs add to the general protection objectives by guaranteeing a repository of hereditary variety.

   Public Commitment and Instruction:

   Zoos effectively connect with people in general in protection through instructive projects, intelligent shows, and effort drives. These endeavors mean to bring issues to light about the difficulties looked by Sumatran tigers and the significance of worldwide preservation.

   Support for In Situ Preservation:

   Numerous zoos designate assets and subsidizing to help in situ preservation projects in the regular environments of Sumatran tigers. This cooperative methodology guarantees an all encompassing technique that consolidates ex situ and in situ protection endeavors.

7. **Progress in Recovery and Delivery Projects: Reestablishing Tigers to Nature**
   Restoration and Delivery Projects Outline:

   Restoration and delivery programs have shown outcome in reestablishing Sumatran tigers to their normal environments.

   Achievement Elements:

   Salvage and Restoration:

   Programs that salvage and restore harmed or stranded Sumatran tigers assume a critical part in their preservation. Veterinary consideration, restoration offices, and conduct preparing add to planning people for discharge.

   Discharge into Safeguarded Regions:

   Fruitful projects include delivering restored tigers into very much safeguarded and reasonable natural surroundings. This guarantees that delivered people get an opportunity to flourish, adding to the wild populace.

   Post-Delivery Observing:

   Thorough post-discharge checking, including satellite following and on-the-ground perceptions, is fundamental to survey the outcome of restoration and delivery programs. Versatile administration in light of checking information adds to the refinement of delivery procedures.

8. **Native Information Mix in Protection: Adjusting Custom and Preservation Native Information Mix Outline:**

In some fruitful protection drives, the joining of native information and practices has demonstrated gainful.

Achievement Variables:

Conventional Biological Information:

Native people group frequently have significant conventional biological information about neighborhood environments, including the way of behaving of natural life like Sumatran tigers. Coordinating this information into preservation methodologies improves the adequacy of protection endeavors.

Local area drove Preservation Practices:

Cooperative endeavors that regard and include native networks in preservation direction engage them to go about as caretakers of their normal environmental factors. This can prompt more economical and socially touchy protection rehearses.

Adjusting Preservation and Social Legacy:

Perceiving the cooperative connection between native societies and the climate, effective drives find some kind of harmony between protection objectives and the conservation of social legacy. This approach encourages an amicable conjunction among people and Sumatran tigers.

9. **Preservation Global's Progress in Tesso Nilo: Promotion and Organizations**

Preservation Global's Tesso Nilo Achievement Outline:

Preservation Global's work in the Tesso Nilo scene embodies the effect of worldwide NGOs in Sumatran tiger protection.

Achievement Variables:

Limit Building and Nearby Associations:

Preservation Worldwide spotlights on building neighborhood limit and shaping associations with legislative offices and nearby networks. This approach guarantees that protection endeavors are educated by neighborhood information and needs.

Backing for Strategy Change:

The association takes part in promotion endeavors to impact strategy changes that favor Sumatran tiger protection. By working with states and policymakers, Preservation Worldwide adds to the creation and implementation of regulations that safeguard tiger living spaces.

Logical Exploration and Observing:

Protection Worldwide accentuates the significance of logical exploration and checking in Tesso Nilo. This remembers reads up for tiger conduct, territory wellbeing, and the effects of human exercises. The information produced illuminates preservation procedures and versatile administration.

7.2 Inspiration for future conservation endeavors.

The triumphs in Sumatran tiger protection offer a reason for festivity as well as a wellspring of motivation for future preservation tries. As we ponder the positive effect of different drives, there arises a guide for the future — a diagram based on local area commitment, imaginative procedures, worldwide joint effort, and a profound regard for nature. In this investigation, we draw motivation from the victories of Sumatran tiger preservation, featuring key components that can direct and persuade future undertakings.

1. **Local area Driven Protection: A Point of support for What's to come**
   One of the resonating illustrations from fruitful Sumatran tiger preservation endeavors is the critical pretended by neighborhood networks. Local area commitment, strengthening, and joint effort have shown to be key parts for maintainable preservation. Drawing motivation from this, future undertakings can embrace the accompanying standards:
   Shared Stewardship:
   The outcome of local area oversaw saves in Kerinci features the force of shared stewardship. Future preservation endeavors can draw motivation from this model by effectively including nearby networks in dynamic cycles, encouraging a feeling of responsibility, and perceiving their job as caretakers of the land.
   Practical Vocations:
   The reconciliation of feasible business programs in preservation, as found in the Harapan Rainforest Task, gives a diagram to what's to come. By setting out financial open doors that line up with protection objectives, future undertakings can diminish reliance on exercises destructive to tiger territories, guaranteeing a mutually beneficial situation for the two individuals and natural life.
   The travel industry as a Protection Device:
   The outcome of eco-the travel industry drives in Kerinci exhibits the capability of the travel industry as a preservation device. Future preservation endeavors can use the travel industry to produce income, bring issues to light, and impart a feeling of obligation among guests, in this way adding to the security of Sumatran tiger natural surroundings.

2. **Creative Techniques: Making ready for Future Preservation**
   Development has been a main thrust behind numerous fruitful Sumatran tiger preservation drives. The reception of state of the art innovations, inventive funding models, and versatile administration techniques fills in as a motivation for future undertakings:
   Supportable Innovation for Checking:
   The utilization of trend setting innovations, for example, camera traps and satellite following, in Kerinci Seblat Public Park embodies the force of advance-ment in checking and safeguarding tiger populaces. Future protection endeav-ors can embrace manageable innovation for improved reconnaissance, constant

information assortment, and quick reaction to criminal operations.

Supportable Funding Models:

The progress of the Harapan Rainforest Venture in mixing protection with monetary interests through economical logging and local area based drives offers an example for what's to come. Future preservation tries can investigate and foster practical supporting models, for example, installment for environment administrations, eco-the travel industry, and carbon credits to make a self-supporting biological system.

Versatile Co-Administration:

The execution of versatile co-administration, as found in the outcome of Kerinci Seblat Public Park, underlines the requirement for adaptability in preservation methodologies. Future undertakings can draw motivation from this methodology by cultivating cooperative dynamic cycles that incorporate neighborhood networks, administrative offices, and progressives, guaranteeing that techniques stay applicable and versatile to evolving conditions.

3. **Worldwide Joint effort: The Strength in Solidarity**

   The Worldwide Tiger Drive (GTI) remains as a demonstration of the force of worldwide joint effort in preservation. Future undertakings can draw motivation from this worldwide exertion by:

   Worldwide Participation:

   Perceiving that the preservation of Sumatran tigers rises above public limits, future undertakings can focus on global participation. Cooperative endeavors between tiger-range nations, global associations, and traditionalists can address transboundary issues, share assets, and intensify the effect of protection drives.

   Interest in Enemy of Poaching Measures:

   The responsibility of GTI part nations to put resources into hostile to poaching estimates fills in as a model for future undertakings. Satisfactory subsidizing, mechanical help, and limit working for policing can altogether decrease poaching episodes and add to the general prosperity of tiger populaces.

   Public Mindfulness and Promotion:

   The GTI's accentuation on open mindfulness and promotion offers a significant illustration for what's to come. Drawing in general society through crusades, instructive projects, and media effort can earn support for preservation drives and make a worldwide local area focused on safeguarding Sumatran tigers.

4. **Movement Projects: Improving Hereditary Variety**

   The outcome of movement programs in Bukit Barisan Selatan Public Park features the significance of hereditary variety in guaranteeing the drawn out feasibility of tiger populaces. Future preservation attempts can draw motivation from this accomplishment by:

   Hereditary Variety Improvement:

   Focusing on hereditary variety in preservation arranging can be a vital concentration for what's in store. Movement endeavors, when painstakingly made due, can add to upgrading hereditary variety and relieving the dangers of inbreeding, guaranteeing better and stronger tiger populaces.

Extensive Territory Insurance:

The progress of movement in Bukit Barisan Selatan Public Park was supplemented by simultaneous endeavors to secure and reestablish tiger environments. Future undertakings can focus on extensive living space insurance, including against poaching measures, local area commitment, and territory rebuilding drives, to establish conditions helpful for moved tigers.

Checking and Versatile Administration:

Thorough post-discharge checking, as found in the movement achievement, gives important information to versatile administration. Future undertakings can accentuate ceaseless observing, integrating innovative progressions, to survey the outcome of preservation systems and refine approaches in light of ongoing data.

5. **Preservation Schooling Drives: Significantly shaping Personalities for What's in store**

The job of zoos, natural life protection focuses, and training drives in molding public discernments and cultivating a feeling of obligation has significant ramifications for what's in store:

Ex Situ Protection and Reproducing Projects:

Future protection endeavors can attract motivation from zoos' interest ex situ preservation. Keeping up with hereditarily different hostage populaces and executing effective rearing projects add to the conservation of the species and give a security net against likely terminations.

Public Commitment and Schooling:

The outcome of zoos in effectively captivating the general population through instructive projects shows the potential for molding a protection cognizant society. Future undertakings can focus on open commitment, utilizing intelligent shows, outreach drives, and instructive organizations to bring issues to light and earn support.

Support for In Situ Preservation:

Perceiving the interconnectedness of in situ and ex situ preservation endeavors, future undertakings can copy the act of numerous zoos in dispensing assets and subsidizing to help protection projects in the regular territories of Sumatran tigers. This cooperative methodology guarantees an all encompassing technique for tiger preservation.

6. **Progress in Recovery and Delivery Projects: An Encouraging sign**

Restoration and delivery programs offer an encouraging sign for the future, displaying the potential for reestablishing Sumatran tigers to their normal natural surroundings. Future preservation attempts can draw motivation from these victories by:

Exhaustive Salvage and Recovery:

Focusing on extensive salvage and recovery programs for harmed or stranded Sumatran tigers can be a foundation of future undertakings. Sufficient veterinary consideration, recovery offices, and social preparation add to the fruitful planning of people for discharge.

Discharge into Very much Safeguarded Natural surroundings:

The outcome of recovery and delivery programs underlines the significance of delivering people into all around secured and reasonable environments. Future undertakings can focus on distinguishing and getting natural surroundings that give ideal circumstances to the renewed introduction of tigers, guaranteeing a higher probability of progress.

Thorough Post-Delivery Observing:

Nonstop post-discharge checking, consolidating satellite following and on-the-ground perceptions, is vital for evaluating the outcome of recovery endeavors. Future undertakings can focus on interest in observing innovation and versatile administration in view of constant information to upgrade the adequacy of delivery programs.

7. **Native Information Joining: A Comprehensive Methodology**

The joining of native information and practices in effective protection drives offers significant experiences for future undertakings:

Regard for Customary Natural Information:

Future protection endeavors can draw motivation from drives that regard and incorporate conventional environmental information. Perceiving the worth of native networks' bits of knowledge into nearby biological systems, including the way of behaving of Sumatran tigers, can upgrade the adequacy of protection procedures.

Local area Drove Protection Practices:

Cooperative endeavors that include and engage native networks in protection navigation can be a core value for what's to come. By regarding and esteeming their commitments, preservation tries can profit from local area drove rehearses that line up with both environmental and social necessities.

Adjusting Preservation and Social Legacy:

The progress of drives that offset protection objectives with the safeguarding of social legacy gives a model to future undertakings. Finding some kind of harmony between the security of regular environments and the social acts of native networks cultivates a more reasonable and conscious way to deal with preservation.

8. **The Job of Global NGOs: Support and Limit Building**

Global NGOs, exemplified by Protection Worldwide's progress in Tesso Nilo, exhibit the effect of promotion and limit building. Future protection attempts can draw motivation by:

Limit Building and Nearby Associations:

Stressing limit constructing and framing organizations with legislative offices and nearby networks can be a foundation for future protection endeavors. This approach guarantees that preservation procedures are established in nearby information, needs, and maintainable practices.

Backing for Strategy Change:

Future protection tries can gain from the promotion endeavors of associations like Preservation Worldwide. Drawing in with policymakers and upholding for strategy changes that favor Sumatran tiger preservation can lastingly affect the lawful systems that safeguard tiger territories.

Logical Exploration and Checking:

The accentuation on logical examination and checking in Tesso Nilo offers a significant example for what's in store. Leading examinations on tiger conduct, territory wellbeing, and the effects of human exercises gives fundamental information to informed navigation and versatile administration.

Chapter 8

The Future Of Sumatran Tigers

As we stand at the junction of the 21st hundred years, the eventual fate of Sumatran tigers remains in a critical state. A basically imperiled subspecies, these glorious animals face a variety of dangers that request pressing and supported preservation endeavors. In this exhaustive investigation, we dig into the difficulties that lie ahead, the procedures expected for their safeguarding, and the general protection objectives that will shape the predetermination of Sumatran tigers.

1. **Current Status and Difficulties**
1. **Populace Decline and Natural surroundings Misfortune:**
   Sumatran tigers, when flourishing across the thick rainforests of Sumatra, presently stand up to a dangerous decrease in populace. The infringement of human exercises, driven by horticultural extension and infrastructural improvement, has prompted significant environment misfortune. Fracture of once touching scenes compounds the weakness of tiger populaces, restricting hereditary variety and thwarting regular ways of behaving like relocation.
2. **Poaching and Unlawful Untamed life Exchange:**
   The relentless danger of poaching and unlawful natural life exchange stays a foreboding shadow over Sumatran tiger preservation. Interest for tiger parts in customary medication and the extraordinary pet exchange drives a worthwhile bootleg market, coming down on the generally lessening populace. The complex organizations engaged with unlawful natural life exchange request powerful global cooperation to destroy and annihilate.
3. **Human-Untamed life Struggle:**
   As human populaces grow, the covering domains among people and tigers increment, prompting heightened human-natural life clashes. Tigers going after domesticated animals can set off retaliatory killings, worsening the generally tricky circumstance for these dominant hunters. Moderating human-untamed

life struggle requires techniques that balance the necessities of neighborhood networks with the basic of tiger protection.

4. **Environmental Change Effects:**

The phantom of environmental change poses a potential threat over Sumatran tigers and their natural surroundings. Climbing temperatures, changed precipitation examples, and outrageous climate occasions compromise the fragile natural equilibrium, affecting prey accessibility and environment reasonableness. Adjusting preservation systems to address these environment initiated difficulties turns into a vital piece of getting a future for Sumatran tigers.

II. Techniques for Future Protection

1. **Living space Insurance and Rebuilding:**
   A key point of support for the fate of Sumatran tigers lies in the security and rebuilding of their territories. The production of interconnected passages and the assignment of safeguarded regions are fundamental for keeping up with practical populaces and working with hereditary trade. Accentuation on reasonable land-use practices and reforestation drives becomes fundamental to check the impacts of territory misfortune.

2. **Reinforcing Hostile to Poaching Measures:**
   The battle against poaching requests increased and key enemy of poaching measures. This incorporates reinforcing policing, high level reconnaissance advances, and cultivating worldwide participation to destroy unlawful natural life exchange organizations. An exhaustive methodology that objectives both the interest and supply sides of the unlawful market is vital for control this danger.

3. **Alleviating Human-Untamed life Struggle:**
   Tending to human-natural life struggle requires a nuanced approach that recognizes and addresses the worries of neighborhood networks. Executing successful clash moderation methodologies, like secure animals fenced in areas, early advance notice frameworks, and remuneration components, cultivates conjunction among people and tigers. Local area commitment and schooling assume a crucial part in building understanding and backing for preservation endeavors.

4. **Environment Strong Protection Methodologies:**

Even with environmental change, protection methodologies should be versatile and tough. This includes recognizing environment refugia, regions that are supposed to remain generally steady, and focusing on these for preservation. Incorporating environment shrewd practices into land-use arranging and protection drives guarantees the drawn out feasibility of Sumatran tiger natural surroundings.

III. Protection Goals for What's in store

1. **Local area Driven Preservation:**
   The eventual fate of Sumatran tigers relies on local area association and strengthening. Protection methodologies should be co-planned with nearby networks, regarding their customary information and guaranteeing that the advantages of preservation straightforwardly add to their prosperity. Feasible occupation choices, instruction, and limit building drives are essential parts of local area driven protection.

2. **Development in Preservation Advances:**
   The quick progressions in innovation offer extraordinary open doors for preservation. Drones, camera traps, satellite checking, and man-made brainpower can change untamed life observing, information assortment, and examination. Embracing these creative innovations upgrades the effectiveness and adequacy of preservation endeavors, giving continuous experiences into tiger conduct, territory wellbeing, and likely dangers.

3. **Worldwide Cooperation and Backing:**
   Sumatran tiger protection can't be bound to public lines; it requests worldwide joint effort. Tiger-range nations, worldwide associations, legislatures, NGOs, and general society should join in backing endeavors. Raising worldwide mindfulness about the predicament of Sumatran tigers and earning support for preservation drives requires maintained and facilitated endeavors on a global scale.

4. **Incorporated Protection Arranging:**
   A coordinated and all encompassing way to deal with protection arranging is basic. This includes coordination between legislative offices, NGOs, neighborhood networks, and different partners to guarantee that protection techniques are thorough and synergistic. Adjusting protection objectives to more extensive improvement plans encourages an amicable harmony between natural safeguarding and human necessities.

5. **Long haul Subsidizing and Monetary Instruments:**

The eventual fate of Sumatran tiger protection depends intensely on getting long haul subsidizing and creating inventive monetary components. Past customary awards, investigating roads, for example, maintainable supporting models, installment for environment administrations, and public-private organizations can make a reasonable financing base. Putting resources into the conservation of biodiversity should be perceived as a fundamental part of worldwide prosperity.

IV. A Dream for What's to come: Concurrence and Flourishing Biological systems

Imagining the eventual fate of Sumatran tigers requires rising above the quick difficulties and embracing an all encompassing vision. In this future:

Concurrence with Nearby People group:

Sumatran tigers coincide agreeably with neighborhood networks, where the two people and untamed life share scenes in a harmonious relationship. Preservation drives focus on the prosperity of nearby inhabitants, guaranteeing that monetary open doors and advantages exude from tiger protection endeavors.

Flourishing Biological systems and Biodiversity:

Safeguarded regions and interconnected scenes support flourishing biological systems. Biodiversity prospers, with Sumatran tigers filling in as umbrella species, showing the strength of whole biological systems. Protection endeavors reach out past tigers to defend the rich woven artwork of vegetation that characterizes Sumatra's exceptional biodiversity.

Creative Advances and Exploration:

State of the art innovations and logical examination consistently illuminate preservation techniques. Constant observing, hereditary examinations, and high level demonstrating procedures add to versatile administration, guaranteeing that protection rehearses stay compelling and receptive to changing ecological circumstances.

Worldwide Joint effort and Promotion:

A worldwide local area joined in its obligation to Sumatran tiger protection effectively participates in promotion and mindfulness crusades. Legislatures, NGOs, and general society team up to dispose of interest for unlawful untamed life items, authorize against poaching measures, and champion arrangements that safeguard tiger living spaces.

Manageable Financing Models:

Manageable supporting models, established in an acknowledgment of the natural worth of biodiversity, give a steady groundwork to preservation drives. These models reserve Sumatran tiger preservation as well as add to more extensive practical advancement objectives, adjusting monetary success to ecological stewardship.

V. A Source of inspiration: Molding the Future Today

The eventual fate of Sumatran tigers isn't foreordained; it is formed by the activities we take today. As caretakers of the Earth, we are shared with the obligation with guarantee that these grand animals keep on wandering the backwoods of Sumatra. The source of inspiration is reverberating:

Individual Commitment:

Each individual plays a part to play in the preservation of Sumatran tigers. Whether through mindful the travel industry, supporting moral associations, or spreading mindfulness, individual activities add to the aggregate exertion.

Strategy Promotion:

Promotion for arrangements that focus on natural life preservation, living space security, and feasible improvement is vital. Drawing in with policymakers, supporting regulation that shields tiger territories, and considering legislatures responsible for their preservation responsibilities are basic advances.

Support for Preservation Associations:

Supporting and effectively captivating with preservation associations is fundamental. These associations assume a vital part in on-the-ground protection endeavors, examination, and promotion. Gifts, chipping in, and coordinated effort fortify their ability to safeguard Sumatran tigers.

Instructive Drives:

Training is a useful asset for change. Coordinating preservation training into school educational plans, cultivating natural proficiency, and advancing public mindfulness crusades add to building a general public that qualities and effectively takes part in the protection of Sumatran tigers.

Capable Utilization:

Tending to the interest for tiger items includes advancing capable utilization. Whether through moral decisions in customary medication or bringing issues to light about the results of untamed life exchange, people can impact request designs that straightforwardly influence the endurance of Sumatran tigers.

VI. A Common Obligation regarding Ages to Come

The fate of Sumatran tigers is a common obligation that rises above limits, societies, and ages. It is a pledge to saving an animal types as well as the multifaceted snare of life that characterizes our planet. As we explore the intricacies of the 21st hundred years, the fate of Sumatran tigers rests in our grasp. Our decisions today decide if these grand animals will persevere as images of strength, flexibility, and the getting through excellence of the regular world. In this common excursion, let our activities reverberation through time, leaving a tradition of conjunction, protection, and a flourishing planet for a long time into the future.

8.1 Examination of the long-term prospects for Sumatran tigers.

The destiny of the Sumatran tiger, a basically jeopardized subspecies, drapes in a dubious equilibrium as it faces a variety of difficulties that undermine its presence. This extensive assessment plunges into the drawn out possibilities for Sumatran tigers, diving into the intricacies of their ongoing circumstance, dissecting the likely difficulties not too far off, investigating open doors for preservation, and illustrating procedures to get a practical future for these radiant animals.

1. **Current Status and Populace Patterns**
1. **Populace Appraisals:**

   Sumatran tigers (Panthera tigris sumatrae) are local to the Indonesian island of Sumatra. Starting around the last solid gauges, the worldwide populace of Sumatran tigers is accepted to be under 400 people, making them one of the most extraordinary and most imperiled large feline species in the world. These tigers are amassed in divided pockets of territory across Sumatra.

2. **Living space Misfortune and Discontinuity:**

   One of the essential dangers to Sumatran tigers is living space misfortune, a result of broad deforestation for farming, logging, and human settlement. The leftover tiger living spaces are progressively divided, disengaging populaces and confining their capacity to meander and keep up with hereditary variety. The development of palm oil ranches, specifically, has been a significant driver of deforestation in Sumatra.

3. **Poaching and Unlawful Untamed life Exchange:**
Poaching stays a critical danger to Sumatran tigers, driven by interest for their body parts in customary medication and the unlawful untamed life exchange. The charm of tiger bones, skins, and other body parts in illegal businesses represents a grave risk to these creatures, with poachers frequently taking advantage of careless policing deficient punishments.

4. **Human-Natural life Struggle:**

As human populaces extend and infringe into tiger natural surroundings, episodes of human-untamed life struggle increment. Tigers going after domesticated animals can prompt retaliatory killings by nearby networks, further compounding the difficulties looked by these dominant hunters. Practical answers for alleviate such contentions are urgent for the conjunction of tigers and neighborhood networks.

II. Future Difficulties and Dangers

1. **Environmental Change Effect:**
Environmental change arises as an approaching danger with significant ramifications for the eventual fate of Sumatran tigers. Changes in precipitation designs, climbing temperatures, and the rising recurrence of outrageous climate occasions present difficulties to the fragile equilibrium of biological systems, influencing both prey accessibility and living space appropriateness. The drawn out results of environmental change on tiger natural surroundings and food sources require versatile preservation systems.

2. **Hereditary Variety Decline:**
The secluded idea of tiger populaces in divided living spaces raises worries about hereditary variety. Inbreeding, a result of restricted quality stream among little populaces, can prompt medical problems and decreased versatility to ecological changes. Keeping up with and improving hereditary variety is essential for the drawn out feasibility of Sumatran tiger populaces.

3. **Framework Improvement Tensions:**
Continuous and arranged foundation advancement projects, like streets and dams, represent extra dangers to Sumatran tigers. These activities can additionally piece living spaces, disturb environmental availability, and increment the gamble of human-tiger clashes. Preservation arranging should coordinate contemplations for foundation improvement to alleviate these possible dangers.

4. **Illness Flare-ups:**

The potential for infection episodes, especially zoonotic sicknesses, represents an inactive danger to Sumatran tigers. Sicknesses sent among people and untamed life can obliterate currently weak populaces. The preservation local area should stay cautious in observing and overseeing potential sickness dangers to defend the wellbeing of tiger populaces.

III. Preservation Potential open doors and Techniques

1. **Territory Insurance and Rebuilding:**
   Integral to the drawn out possibilities of Sumatran tigers is the insurance and rebuilding of their normal territories. This includes the foundation and upkeep of safeguarded regions, passages to interface separated environments, and reforestation drives. Cooperative endeavors between legislative organizations, NGOs, and neighborhood networks are fundamental for the outcome of natural surroundings preservation.

2. **Fortifying Enemy of Poaching Measures:**
   Combatting poaching requires a complex methodology that incorporates fortifying policing, high level reconnaissance innovations, and destroying unlawful natural life exchange organizations. Worldwide cooperation is crucial for address the worldwide interest for tiger parts and guarantee powerful requirement of hostile to poaching measures.

3. **Relieving Human-Natural life Struggle:**
   Long haul concurrence among tigers and nearby networks requires powerful procedures to alleviate human-untamed life struggle. This incorporates the advancement of secure domesticated animals fenced in areas, early advance notice frameworks, and remuneration components for misfortunes caused because of tiger predation. Local area commitment and schooling assume a urgent part in building understanding and backing for such moderation endeavors.

4. **Environment Strong Protection Systems:**
   Adjusting to the effects of environmental change requires the coordination of environment strong protection procedures. Distinguishing and safeguarding environment refugia, regions expected to remain somewhat stable notwithstanding environmental change, becomes urgent. Protection arranging should be adaptable and versatile, taking into account the powerful idea of changing environment conditions.

5. **Network and Hereditary Variety Improvement:**
   Guaranteeing the hereditary soundness of Sumatran tiger populaces includes improving availability between divided natural surroundings. This might incorporate the formation of natural passageways that work with the development of tigers across scenes. Movement programs, directed by hereditary investigations, can likewise add to the improvement of hereditary variety.

6. **Practical Advancement Arranging:**

Offsetting monetary advancement with protection goals is fundamental for the drawn out conjunction of tigers and people. Feasible improvement arranging includes incorporating protection into land-use choices, advancing eco-accommodating practices, and utilizing financial models that focus on both natural conservation and human prosperity.

IV. Cooperative Drives and Worldwide Help

1. **Worldwide Tiger Drive:**
   Worldwide drives, like the Worldwide Tiger Drive (GTI), assume a vital part in organizing endeavors to moderate tiger populaces across their reach nations.
   The GTI centers around resolving main points of interest like poaching, natural surroundings misfortune, and human-untamed life struggle through cooperation, limit building, and support.

2. **NGO and Government Associations:**
   Associations between non-administrative associations (NGOs) and legislative organizations are instrumental in executing successful preservation techniques. These associations frequently include limit building, logical examination, local area commitment, and strategy promotion. Cooperation guarantees an exhaustive and synergistic way to deal with preservation.

3. **Examination and Checking Organizations:**
   Logical examination and checking networks contribute essential information for informed dynamic in preservation. Cooperative endeavors including specialists, traditionalists, and administrative organizations assist with following tiger populaces, figure out their way of behaving, and survey the adequacy of preservation intercessions. Worldwide participation improves the extension and effect of these exploration drives.

4. **Protection The travel industry and Public Commitment:**

Protection the travel industry, when dependably made due, can contribute both monetarily and through mindfulness building. Connecting with people in general in protection endeavors encourages a feeling of obligation and produces support for tiger preservation. Public mindfulness crusades, instructive projects, and ecotourism drives can add to a worldwide local area put resources into the drawn out endurance of Sumatran tigers.

V. The Job of Innovation and Advancement

1. **High level Observing Advances:**
   The appearance of trend setting innovations offers additional opportunities for checking and safeguarding Sumatran tigers. Camera traps, satellite following, and other remote detecting advancements give important bits of knowledge into tiger conduct, territory wellbeing, and expected dangers. The coordination of

these advances into preservation techniques upgrades the accuracy and effectiveness of checking endeavors.

2. **Hereditary Exploration and Preservation:**
   Progressions in hereditary examination give devices to surveying and dealing with the hereditary variety of tiger populaces. Hereditary investigations illuminate movement programs, recognize key populaces for preservation concentration, and guide endeavors to moderate the effects of inbreeding. This information is urgent for guaranteeing the drawn out practicality of Sumatran tiger populaces.

3. **Public Commitment through Computerized Stages:**

Computerized stages and web-based entertainment offer extraordinary open doors for public commitment and promotion. Protection associations influence these stages to bring issues to light, accumulate support, and instruct general society about the situation of Sumatran tigers. Online missions add to building a worldwide local area focused on tiger protection.

VI. Schooling and Mindfulness Drives

1. **Protection Training in Schools:**
   Coordinating protection training into school educational programs encourages a feeling of natural stewardship since the beginning. Youngsters taught about the significance of biodiversity, biological systems, and the job of tigers in keeping up with environmental equilibrium are bound to become advocates for preservation later on.

2. **Local area Based Ecological Instruction:**
   Local area based ecological training drives enable nearby networks with information about the worth of untamed life, the significance of biodiversity, and the job they play in preservation. These drives advance a feeling of pride and obligation among local area individuals, prompting more feasible preservation rehearses.

3. **Media and Expressions for Preservation:**

Media, including narratives, movies, and craftsmanship, assumes a urgent part in forming public discernments and perspectives towards protection. Imaginative undertakings that feature the magnificence of Sumatran tigers, their significance in environments, and the difficulties they face add to building a more extensive voting demographic for tiger protection.

VII. Future Situations and Protection Real factors

1. **Hopeful Situation:**
   In a hopeful situation, coordinated and compelling protection endeavors lead to the adjustment and recuperation of Sumatran tiger populaces. Living space

security and reclamation drives prevail with regards to making interconnected scenes that help solid environments. Hostile to poaching estimates check unlawful natural life exchange, and human-untamed life struggle moderation techniques cultivate concurrence among tigers and neighborhood networks. Hereditary variety is upgraded through designated movement projects, and environment versatile protection rehearses guarantee the flexibility of tiger populaces.

2. **Cynical Situation:**

In a cynical situation, proceeded with living space misfortune, poaching, and lacking protection estimates lead to a further decrease in Sumatran tiger populaces. Divided territories bring about disengaged and innate populaces, undermining their capacity to adjust to changing natural circumstances. Human-natural life struggle raises, disintegrating support for tiger preservation among nearby networks. Environmental change fuels existing difficulties, driving tigers nearer to the edge of annihilation.

VIII. A Source of inspiration for Long haul Protection

1. **Fortifying Legitimate Systems:**
   The foundation and authorization of powerful legitimate structures are fundamental for long haul tiger preservation. This incorporates severe punishments for poaching, natural surroundings obliteration, and unlawful untamed life exchange. Legitimate measures should likewise resolve issues connected with land-use arranging, foundation improvement, and the security of basic tiger living spaces.

2. **Scene Level Preservation Arranging:**
   Preservation arranging should work at a scene level, taking into account the interconnectedness of territories and the assorted requirements of various partners. Cooperative endeavors between administrative offices, NGOs, nearby networks, and the confidential area are fundamental for creating and executing exhaustive scene level preservation plans.

3. **Versatile Administration and Exploration:**
   Versatile administration, informed by progressing examination and checking, is critical to the drawn out outcome of preservation drives. Customary appraisals of tiger populaces, environment wellbeing, and the adequacy of preservation systems take into consideration changes and refinements. Putting resources into nonstop exploration guarantees that preservation rehearses stay versatile and receptive to arising difficulties.

4. **Practical Supporting Systems:**
   Long haul protection endeavors require supportable funding systems that go past transient awards. Investigating imaginative monetary models, for example, installment for biological system administrations, manageable the travel

industry, and public-private organizations, can make a steady financing base. Incorporating protection into more extensive supportable advancement plans upgrades the reasonability of these monetary instruments.

5. **Worldwide Participation and Discretion:**
The preservation of Sumatran tigers rises above public lines, requesting global collaboration and strategy. Tiger-range nations, fully backed by the global local area, should team up to address transboundary issues, for example, unlawful untamed life exchange, environment assurance, and environmental change. Conciliatory endeavors can guarantee that common preservation objectives are focused on provincial and worldwide plans.

6. **Engaging Nearby People group:**
Engaging neighborhood networks as stewards of their regular assets is crucial to the drawn out progress of tiger protection. This includes giving maintainable business choices, guaranteeing that preservation benefits straightforwardly add to nearby prosperity, and cultivating a deep satisfaction and possession in the security of Sumatran tigers.

7. **Public Commitment and Support:**

Building a worldwide voting demographic for Sumatran tiger preservation depends on open commitment and promotion. Preservation associations, states, and people should effectively take part in mindfulness crusades, instructive drives, and backing endeavors. Public strain can impact strategy choices, drive monetary help, and raise the significance of tiger preservation on the worldwide plan.

8.2 Discussion on the importance of continued conservation efforts and the role of global collaboration.

The continuous situation of Sumatran tigers, a fundamentally jeopardized sub-species, requires a supported obligation to preservation endeavors. As we explore the 21st 100 years, the significance of saving biodiversity, safeguarding environments, and guaranteeing the endurance of notorious species like the Sumatran tiger couldn't possibly be more significant. This conversation digs into the basic job of proceeded with protection endeavors and the meaning of worldwide coordinated effort in getting a future for these superb animals.

1. **The Basic of Proceeded with Protection Endeavors**
1. **Biodiversity Protection:**
The Sumatran tiger, Panthera tigris sumatrae, fills in as an umbrella species, representing the strength of the environments it possesses. Biodiversity is the bedrock of environmental equilibrium, and the preservation of lead species like the Sumatran tiger has flowing impacts on the horde greenery that comprise these many-sided biological systems. Safeguarding biodiversity guarantees the flexibility and versatility of biological systems to natural changes.

2. **Biological Equilibrium and Trophic Fountains:**
   Tigers, as dominant hunters, assume a vital part in keeping up with biological equilibrium through trophic fountains. Their presence directs prey populaces, forestalling overgrazing and permitting vegetation to thrive. This, thusly, has flowing consequences for different species reliant upon these biological systems. Disturbances in the populace elements of tigers can prompt lopsided characteristics, influencing whole food networks and environment wellbeing.

3. **Biological system Administrations and Human Prosperity:**
   Sound environments give a bunch of administrations pivotal for human prosperity, from clean air and water to fertilization of harvests and environment guideline. The protection of Sumatran tigers adds to the safeguarding of these biological system administrations. Supporting these administrations isn't just imperative for the networks living in vicinity to tiger territories yet in addition for worldwide ecological solidness.

4. **Logical Exploration and Biological Comprehension:**

Preservation endeavors including Sumatran tigers contribute essentially to logical examination and natural comprehension. Concentrating on tiger conduct, territory necessities, and the interconnectedness of biological systems offers important experiences that reach out past individual species. This information is central for informed preservation procedures, versatile administration, and tending to more extensive ecological difficulties.

II. The Job of Worldwide Coordinated effort in Protection

1. **Transboundary Nature of Preservation Difficulties:**
   Preserving Sumatran tigers is innately a transboundary try. The difficulties they face — living space misfortune, poaching, and environmental change — rise above public boundaries. Successful protection requires cooperation between various locales inside Sumatra as well as between tiger-range nations, perceiving the interconnected idea of biological frameworks.

2. **Shared Liability regarding Worldwide Biodiversity:**
   The worldwide local area shares an aggregate liability regarding the protection of biodiversity. Sumatran tigers, as a leader animal groups, represent the interconnectedness of environments and the effect of human exercises on far off natural life. Worldwide coordinated effort recognizes that the destiny of Sumatran tigers is entwined with more extensive worldwide protection objectives and mirrors a pledge to shared stewardship.

3. **Global Settlements and Arrangements:**
   Global settlements and arrangements give systems to cooperative protection endeavors. Shows like the Show on Natural Variety (CBD) and the Show on Worldwide Exchange Jeopardized Types of Wild Fauna and Verdure (Refers

to) work with participation between nations to resolve issues connected with biodiversity preservation, including the security of imperiled species like the Sumatran tiger.

4. **Protection Financing and Asset Assignment:**

Worldwide joint effort reaches out to the monetary help expected for protection drives. Global financing from legislative bodies, non-administrative associations (NGOs), and magnanimous establishments assumes a critical part in designating assets for on-the-ground protection endeavors. This monetary help helps span holes in subsidizing for drives going from natural surroundings assurance to against poaching measures.

III. Worldwide Joint effort in real life: Examples of overcoming adversity

1. **The Worldwide Tiger Drive:**
   The Worldwide Tiger Drive (GTI) remains as a demonstration of the effect of worldwide coordinated effort in tiger protection. Sent off in 2008, the GTI unites tiger-range nations, worldwide associations, and partners to address the critical dangers confronting wild tigers. Its objectives incorporate multiplying the quantity of wild tigers by 2022, improving tiger territories, and controling unlawful exchange. The GTI features the force of facilitated endeavors in tending to complex preservation challenges.

2. **Preservation Worldwide's Endeavors in Tesso Nilo:**
   Preservation Worldwide's work in the Tesso Nilo scene in Sumatra embodies the cooperative energy between worldwide joint effort and neighborhood activity. By collaborating with nearby networks, legislative offices, and global partners, Preservation Worldwide plays had a vital impact in safeguarding basic tiger living spaces. Their incorporated methodology includes logical exploration, local area commitment, and strategy backing, exhibiting the adequacy of all encompassing protection procedures.

3. **The Sumatran Tiger Recovery and Delivery Program:**

Transboundary cooperation is likewise obvious in the Sumatran Tiger Restoration and Delivery Program, a joint drive including Indonesia and Malaysia. The program centers around restoring and delivering seized or harmed tigers back into nature. The cooperative idea of the program features the significance of shared mastery, assets, and an aggregate obligation to the preservation of this jeopardized species.

IV. Difficulties and Open doors in Worldwide Cooperation

1. **Challenges:**
   Notwithstanding the triumphs, worldwide coordinated effort in tiger protection faces difficulties that warrant consideration. These difficulties incorporate

international strains, contrasting public needs, and variations in monetary commitments. Conquering these difficulties requires conciliatory endeavors, compelling correspondence, and a common acknowledgment of the interconnected idea of ecological issues.

2. **Potential open doors:**

Potential open doors for upgraded worldwide coordinated effort flourish. Innovative progressions, like remote detecting and satellite observing, work with ongoing information sharing and cooperative examination. The ascent of web-based entertainment and advanced stages empowers the worldwide local area to participate in protection backing and mindfulness building. Utilizing these open doors reinforces the aggregate effect of protection drives.

V. The Job of Innovation in Worldwide Coordinated effort

1. **Information Sharing and Remote Detecting:**
   Innovation assumes a critical part in worldwide cooperation through information sharing and remote detecting. Satellite symbolism and remote detecting advances give constant information on environment changes, deforestation, and infringements. This common data upgrades the capacity of different partners to screen and answer arising dangers, encouraging a cooperative and informed way to deal with preservation.

2. **Resident Science and Local area Commitment:**
   Resident science drives, worked with by computerized stages, draw in a worldwide crowd in preservation endeavors. From natural life checking applications to online stages for revealing ecological infringement, innovation enables people overall to add to preservation. This democratization of information assortment fortifies the grassroots part of worldwide cooperation.

3. **Computerized Promotion and Mindfulness:**

Computerized stages act as useful assets for support and mindfulness. Protection associations influence virtual entertainment, digital recordings, and online missions to bring issues to light about the difficulties confronting Sumatran tigers. Worldwide crowds can effectively take part in protection discoursed, support drives monetarily, and pressure policymakers to focus on tiger preservation.

VI. The Moral Element of Worldwide Joint effort

1. **Moral Contemplations in Protection:**
   Worldwide cooperation in protection endeavors should be supported by moral contemplations. This incorporates regarding the privileges and points of view of neighborhood networks, recognizing the effect of preservation choices on their vocations, and guaranteeing that the advantages of protection are evenhandedly

dispersed. Moral coordinated effort requires straightforwardness, inclusivity, and a promise to equity.

2. **Native Information and Neighborhood Intelligence:**

Consolidating native information and nearby insight is fundamental to moral worldwide joint effort. Native people group frequently have significant experiences into the biology and conduct of species like the Sumatran tiger. Regarding and incorporating this information into protection techniques improves the viability of drives as well as cultivates a feeling of responsibility and participation.

VII. A Source of inspiration: Reinforcing Worldwide Cooperation

1. **Tact and Political Will:**
   Reinforcing worldwide cooperation requires discretionary endeavors and political will. Tiger-range nations should focus on preservation in their public plans, perceiving the common obligation regarding safeguarding biodiversity. Conciliatory exchanges and arrangements ought to zero in on conquering international difficulties and cultivating a feeling of collaboration.

2. **Comprehensive Independent direction:**
   Comprehensive dynamic cycles are crucial for compelling worldwide coordinated effort. Counting delegates from nearby networks, native gatherings, NGOs, and administrative organizations in dynamic discussions guarantees that different points of view are thought of. This inclusivity cultivates a feeling of shared liability and improves the probability of effective preservation results.

3. **Development in Financing Models:**
   Creative subsidizing models can upgrade worldwide coordinated effort by broadening and growing monetary assets for preservation. Investigating instruments, for example, obligation for-nature trades, influence effective money management, and public-private organizations can make practical subsidizing streams. This development in financing adjusts preservation to more extensive monetary interests, earning support from different partners.

4. **Outfitting Innovation for Preservation:**
   Proceeded with progressions in innovation offer remarkable open doors for coordinated effort. Reinforcing networks for information sharing, utilizing man-made consciousness for environmental demonstrating, and upgrading correspondence through computerized stages are roads to saddle innovation for protection. Coordinating these instruments into cooperative drives upgrades proficiency and the effect of worldwide preservation endeavors.

5. **Training and Support:**

Schooling and support assume essential parts in fortifying worldwide coordinated effort. Public mindfulness crusades, instructive projects, and promotion endeavors advise people about the significance regarding Sumatran tiger protection. A very much educated worldwide populace is bound to help and take part in cooperative drives, coming down on states and associations to effectively focus on preservation.

Chapter 9

Conclusion

The excursion through the huge scenes of Sumatra, following the strides of the fundamentally jeopardized Sumatran tiger, has been one set apart by difficulties, strength, and the steadfast responsibility of people, networks, associations, and countries. This legendary story of endurance unfurls against a background of environment misfortune, poaching dangers, human-untamed life clashes, and the approaching phantom of environmental change. As we arrive at the finish of this investigation, the embroidery woven is one of earnestness, shared liability, and the potential for extraordinary change.

1. **Considering the Preservation Scene**
1. **The Delicacy of Sumatran Tigers' Presence:**
   The distinct reality confronting Sumatran tigers is one of outrageous weakness. With less than 400 people left in the wild, these superb animals are at the cliff of eradication. Environment misfortune, powered by rural development and deforestation, has cut scars into their once-broad domains. Poaching, driven by interest for their body parts, undermines the actual center of their reality. Human-natural life clashes add one more layer of intricacy, imperiling the two tigers and nearby networks.
2. **Preservation Drives as Encouraging signs:**

Despite misfortune, protection drives arise as encouraging signs. From the rich scenes of the Tesso Nilo district to transboundary recovery programs, these undertakings embody the versatility of Sumatran tigers and the commitment of those endeavoring to guarantee their endurance. The multi-layered approach including natural surroundings insurance, hostile to poaching measures, local area commitment, and global cooperation highlights the interconnectedness of preservation endeavors.

II. The Basic of Proceeded with Preservation Endeavors

1. **Biodiversity Conservation:**
   The preservation of Sumatran tigers rises above the security of a solitary animal groups. It is a promise to protecting biodiversity, perceiving that every part of the biological system adds to its strength and usefulness. The Sumatran tiger, as a dominant hunter, holds an exceptional natural job, impacting the elements of prey populaces and keeping a fragile equilibrium that reverberates all through the snare of life.

2. **Environmental Agreement and Human Prosperity:**
   The call for proceeded with protection endeavors reverberates for the tiger as well as for the prosperity of human networks and the more extensive biological system. Sound environments, sustained by the presence of dominant hunters like the Sumatran tiger, offer fundamental types of assistance like clean air, water, and fertilization. The interconnectedness of environmental agreement and human prosperity highlights the significance of supporting these essential scenes.

3. **Logical Request and Environmental Insight:**

Protection endeavors are not simply demonstrations of conservation but rather progressing potential open doors for logical request and environmental insight. The investigation of Sumatran tigers adds to how we might interpret complex biological systems, offering experiences into natural connections, biodiversity elements, and the effects of human exercises. In this pursuit, science and customary biological information merge, making a comprehensive way to deal with protection.

III. Worldwide Coordinated effort as a Foundation of Preservation Achievement

1. **Rising above Boundaries for Tiger Preservation:**
   The Sumatran tiger, as a leader animal categories, requests a cooperative methodology that rises above borders. The difficulties looked by these tigers, from living space discontinuity to the unlawful untamed life exchange, recognize no international limits. Worldwide cooperation, exemplified by drives like the Worldwide Tiger Drive, perceives the common obligation of countries and the worldwide local area in protecting worldwide biodiversity.

2. **Shared Liability regarding Biodiversity:**
   The common obligation regarding biodiversity protection isn't restricted to tiger-range nations alone. It reaches out to the worldwide local area, where the effects of human exercises resound across mainlands. Sumatran tigers represent the interconnectedness of biological systems and the significant effect of aggregate human decisions. By recognizing this common obligation, we prepare for cooperative arrangements that address the underlying drivers of biodiversity misfortune.

3. Global Settlements and Arrangements:

The system for worldwide cooperation is invigorated by global deals and arrangements. Shows like the Show on Natural Variety (CBD) and the Show on Global Exchange Jeopardized Types of Wild Fauna and Vegetation (Refers to) give roads to composed activity. These arrangements highlight the requirement for aggregate endeavors to battle unlawful natural life exchange, safeguard basic environments, and guarantee the endurance of jeopardized species like the Sumatran tiger.

IV. Worldwide Coordinated effort in real life: Examples of overcoming adversity and Difficulties

1. **Wins of Worldwide Cooperation:**
   Inside the domain of worldwide cooperation, examples of overcoming adversity arise as directing lights. The Worldwide Tiger Drive's aggressive objectives of multiplying wild tiger populaces and improving living spaces exhibit the potential for purposeful endeavors to impact positive change. Drives by associations, for example, Preservation Worldwide and cooperative projects like the Sumatran Tiger Recovery and Delivery Program grandstand the unmistakable effect of worldwide coordinated effort on the ground.

2. **Provokes on the Way to Joint effort:**

In any case, the way to worldwide cooperation isn't without challenges. International pressures, contrasting public needs, and differences in monetary commitments present impressive hindrances. Defeating these difficulties requests conciliatory artfulness, straightforward correspondence, and a common acknowledgment of the earnestness and gravity of the protection emergency. Worldwide joint effort should explore these intricacies to make supported progress.

V. Innovation and Development: Impetuses for Protection

1. **Mechanical Progressions in Protection:**
   Innovation arises as a strong impetus for preservation, offering imaginative answers for age-old difficulties. Remote detecting innovations, satellite checking, and high level camera traps give phenomenal bits of knowledge into tiger environments and conduct. These devices upgrade the accuracy of preservation systems, considering continuous observing and versatile administration.

2. **Resident Science and Computerized Support:**

The democratization of protection through resident science and advanced backing enhances the aggregate effect of worldwide cooperation. From untamed life checking applications that draw in people in general in information assortment to online missions that bring issues to light, innovation changes people into dynamic members in the protection story. The combination of computerized stages and protection support makes a worldwide local area put resources into the destiny of Sumatran tigers.

VI. The Moral Component of Preservation and Cooperation

1. **Moral Contemplations in Protection:**
   In the midst of the quest for protection objectives, moral contemplations should direct every choice and activity. The freedoms of neighborhood networks, the incorporation of native information, and the fair dispersion of preservation benefits stand as mainstays of moral protection. Straightforwardness, inclusivity, and equity are major to building a preservation system that regards both nature and humankind.

2. **Native Insight and Social Safeguarding:**

Integrating native insight into protection techniques isn't just morally basic yet in addition fundamental for the safeguarding of assorted societies. Native people group frequently have significant natural bits of knowledge that have supported biodiversity for ages. Perceiving and regarding these commitments cultivates a cooperative ethos that respects both social variety and natural respectability.

VII. Exploring What's to come: An Aggregate Source of inspiration

1. **Tact and Political Will:**
   Exploring the eventual fate of Sumatran tigers requires steadfast discretion and political will. Tiger-range nations should focus on protection in their strategy plans, perceiving the drawn out benefits for the two environments and neighborhood networks. Political endeavors ought to rise above international contrasts, cultivating cooperation for a common worldwide legacy.

2. **Fortifying Comprehensive Navigation:**
   Comprehensive dynamic stands as a foundation for future protection tries. Counting agents from neighborhood networks, native gatherings, NGOs, and administrative organizations guarantees that different points of view are thought of. This inclusivity improves the viability of protection methodologies as well as encourages a feeling of shared liability.

3. **Developing Financing Models for Manageability:**
   Economical protection endeavors require inventive subsidizing models that guarantee monetary suitability past transient awards. Investigating systems, for example, installment for environment administrations, influence financial planning, and public-private organizations makes a steady subsidizing base. Coordinating preservation into more extensive feasible improvement plans upgrades the practicality of these monetary components.

4. **Outfitting Innovation for Protection 2.0:**
   As innovation keeps on propelling, its part in protection should advance. Outfitting Innovation 2.0 includes improving existing devices as well as embracing arising advancements like man-made brainpower, blockchain, and large information examination. These advancements hold the possibility to reform preservation procedures, from anticipating poaching examples to upgrading living space rebuilding endeavors.

5. **Enabling Neighborhood People group:**

Enabling neighborhood networks arises as a key part for fruitful protection. Reasonably coordinating nearby networks into the protection story includes giving elective livelihoods, guaranteeing impartial sharing of advantages, and encouraging a feeling of pride. The strengthening of neighborhood stewards changes them into partners in the common mission of safeguarding Sumatran tigers and their territories.

VIII. The Unfurling Embroidered artwork of Trust

In this closing part, we stand at the nexus of difficulties and open doors, confronted with the obligation of forming the fate of Sumatran tigers and the biological systems they occupy. The embroidery woven through the investigation of continuous preservation drives, worldwide cooperation, mechanical developments, and moral contemplations is an intricate mosaic that mirrors the criticalness of our common protection venture.

As we explore the complex strings of this embroidery, an aggregate source of inspiration resounds — a call that reverberations through the halls of time. The destiny of Sumatran tigers is weaved with our decisions, choices, and the profundity of our obligation to a practical and amicable concurrence with the normal world. The basic for proceeded with preservation endeavors is clear, directed by the rule that the insurance of one animal types resounds across the whole trap of life.

In the unfurling embroidery of trust, every person, local area, association, and country plays a part to play. It is a cooperative orchestra where the tune of preservation is created by the aggregate voices and activities of a worldwide local area devoted to supporting life in the entirety of its structures.

IX. A Dream for Later

As we imagine the future, let it be one where Sumatran tigers wander unreservedly across rejuvenated scenes, where their thunders reverberation through reestablished woodlands, and where the fragile equilibrium of biological systems is safeguarded for a long time into the future. A future where worldwide cooperation isn't just an idea however a resided reality, where innovation is a power for environmental recovery, and where moral contemplations guide each choice on the way of preservation.

Let the vision for later be one where the preservation heritage we pass on isn't simply a demonstration of the flexibility of Sumatran tigers yet a demonstration of the strength of the human soul — a soul equipped for rising above limits, encouraging sympathy, and protecting the indispensable marvels of our common planet.

In the soul of trust, responsibility, and shared liability, let us set out on the excursion that lies ahead. For in the assurance of Sumatran tigers, we secure their future as well as the fate of a planet that blossoms with the complex dance of biodiversity — a dance that welcomes every one of us to be dynamic members, stewards, and watchmen of the exceptional embroidery of life.

9.1 Recapitulation of the unique status and importance of Sumatran tigers.

As we dig further into the many-sided domains of Sumatra's rainforests and take apart the multi-layered difficulties looked by the fundamentally imperiled Sumatran tiger, it becomes vital to restate the special status and significance these lofty animals hold. Past their magnetic charm, Sumatran tigers epitomize a cornerstone animal varieties, an environmental key part whose endurance resounds across the rich embroidery of biodiversity, human prosperity, and worldwide protection objectives.

1. **The Unique case and Problematic Status of Sumatran Tigers**
1. **Fundamentally Jeopardized Characterization:**
   The Global Association for Protection of Nature (IUCN) arranges Sumatran tigers (Panthera tigris sumatrae) as fundamentally jeopardized — the most noteworthy gamble level on the annihilation range. With an expected populace of less than 400 people staying in the wild, the Sumatran tiger's status highlights the earnestness of protection endeavors to turn away their up and coming eradication.
2. **Novel Subspecies of Tiger:**

Among the different subspecies of tigers, the Sumatran tiger stands apart as an unmistakable and one of a kind substance. More modest in size contrasted with its partners, it shows variations fit to the thick rainforests of Sumatra. With a hazier and thicker coat decorated with striking orange stripes, the Sumatran tiger is a lovely sign of developmental dissimilarity, a demonstration of the variety inside the tiger heredity.

II. Environmental Meaning of Sumatran Tigers

1. **Cornerstone Species in Biological systems:**
   Sumatran tigers expect the job of a cornerstone animal varieties inside their environments. As dominant hunters, they control prey populaces, forestalling overgrazing and permitting vegetation to prosper.
   This flowing impact stretches out to various species inside the biological system, molding the elements of vegetation. The deficiency of this dominant hunter can disturb these sensitive adjusts, prompting natural repercussions.
2. **Keeping up with Biodiversity and Biological system Wellbeing:**

The presence of Sumatran tigers is naturally connected to biodiversity and environment wellbeing. By controlling the populaces of herbivores, they in a roundabout way add to the upkeep of plant variety. Solid environments, thus, support heap species, from bugs to birds, making an amicable transaction that guarantees the strength of the whole biological system.

III. Social and Emblematic Significance

1. **Social Importance in Sumatra:**
   Sumatran tigers hold profound social importance in the hearts and customs of individuals of Sumatra. Implanted in neighborhood fables, workmanship, and otherworldly convictions, these great animals are woven into the social texture of the island. Their presence rises above the domains of the physical, becoming emblematic portrayals of solidarity, secret, and the sensitive balance among mankind and nature.

2. **Image of Preservation Difficulties:**

On a more extensive scale, Sumatran tigers have become representative symbols of the preservation challenges looked by huge carnivores internationally. Their battle for endurance typifies the more extensive dangers of natural surroundings misfortune, poaching, and human-untamed life struggle that influence numerous species across assorted biological systems. The protection story encompassing Sumatran tigers fills in as a mobilizing point for worldwide consideration and activity.

IV. Financial Worth and Ecotourism Potential

1. **Financial Commitments to Ecotourism:**
   Past their biological and social importance, Sumatran tigers have the potential for financial commitments through ecotourism. The appeal of experiencing these slippery large felines right at home can draw sightseers, giving monetary motivations to neighborhood networks and state run administrations to put resources into tiger protection. Appropriately oversaw ecotourism drives can make an economical wellspring of financing for protection endeavors.

2. **Biological system Administrations and Financial Solidness:**

The biological system administrations given by unblemished tiger environments add to monetary steadiness for a bigger scope. From watershed security to environment guideline, these administrations have unmistakable monetary worth.

The protection of Sumatran tigers and their natural surroundings, subsequently, converts into long haul benefits for the more extensive economy, underlining the interconnectedness of preservation and financial prosperity.

V. Difficulties to the Exceptional Status of Sumatran Tigers

1. **Living space Misfortune and Fracture:**
   The principal challenge to the novel status of Sumatran tigers is the steady misfortune and discontinuity of their environments. Deforestation driven by agribusiness, logging, and framework advancement has cut profound entry points into once-coterminous rainforests. This living space misfortune confines tiger populaces, prompting expanded weakness and compounding the gamble of inbreeding.

2. **Poaching and Unlawful Natural life Exchange:**
   Poaching stays an unavoidable danger, energized by the interest for tiger body parts in customary medication and as superficial points of interest. The unlawful natural life exchange imperils individual tigers as well as propagates the pattern of interest, driving further poaching. Endeavors to control this illegal exchange are basic for the endurance of Sumatran tigers.

3. **Human-Natural life Struggle:**

As human populaces infringe upon tiger environments, clashes definitely emerge. Human-natural life struggle represents a double danger — imperiling the two tigers and neighborhood networks. Retaliatory killings, frequently powered by dread or monetary misfortune, heighten the difficulties looked by Sumatran tigers and highlight the requirement for successful moderation procedures.

VI. Preservation Drives as Encouraging signs

1. **Incorporated Protection Approaches:**
   In spite of the impressive difficulties, various protection drives stand as encouraging signs. Coordinated approaches that join natural surroundings insurance, local area commitment, hostile to poaching measures, and worldwide cooperation are yielding positive results. Models incorporate safeguarded regions, restoration programs, and feasible advancement projects that fit human necessities with tiger preservation.

2. **Transboundary Cooperation:**

The transboundary idea of Sumatran tiger environments requires cooperative endeavors across borders. Drives like the Sumatran Tiger Restoration and Delivery Program, which includes both Indonesia and Malaysia, epitomize the capability of worldwide collaboration.

Such joint efforts are vital for making interconnected scenes that take into account the normal development and quality progression of tiger populaces.

VII. The Job of Innovation in Protection

1. **Mechanical Advancements for Checking:**
   Innovation has arisen as an essential partner in the preservation tool stash.

High level observing innovations, including satellite symbolism, camera traps, and remote detecting, empower ongoing following of tiger populaces and their environments. This information driven approach upgrades the accuracy of protection techniques, working with designated intercessions where they are generally required.

2. **Advanced Promotion and Public Commitment:**

Computerized stages assume an extraordinary part in preservation backing. Virtual entertainment, online missions, and advanced narrating intensify the voices supporting for Sumatran tigers. These stages draw in a worldwide crowd, encouraging mindfulness, earning support, and preparing public strain on states and associations to focus on tiger preservation.

VIII. Moral Contemplations in Preservation

1. **Native Information and Nearby Insight:**
   A moral way to deal with preservation perceives the significance of native information and nearby insight. Native people group frequently have profound environmental experiences that can illuminate and advance preservation methodologies. Regarding and consolidating this customary information improves the viability of drives as well as cultivates a feeling of shared stewardship.

2. **Comprehensive Direction:**

Comprehensive dynamic cycles are essential to moral preservation. Neighborhood people group, native gatherings, and different partners should pull up a chair at the table, it are considered to guarantee that assorted viewpoints. This inclusivity not just regards the privileges of those straightforwardly affected by preservation gauges yet in addition upgrades the authenticity and viability of drives.

IX. The Way ahead: Adjusting Preservation and Improvement

1. **Manageable Turn of events and Preservation Cooperative energy:**
   The way ahead requires a fragile harmony between preservation goals and the necessities of developing human populaces. Reasonable improvement rehearses that fit monetary advancement with biological trustworthiness offer a way forward. This collaboration recognizes that the prosperity of the two people and tigers is interlaced, requiring arrangements that benefit both.

2. **Engaging Neighborhood People group:**

Engaging neighborhood networks arises as a key part for economical protection. Through people group based preservation models, neighborhood inhabitants become dynamic members and stewards of their normal legacy. This strengthening includes giving elective occupations, guaranteeing fair sharing of advantages, and cultivating a feeling of concurrence with untamed life.

9.2 Call to action for readers to contribute to the conservation of these magnificent creatures and their rainforest habitat.

The situation of Sumatran tigers, wavering near the very edge of termination, requests an earnest and aggregate reaction. As we explore the complex trap of difficulties confronting these grand animals and their rainforest environment, the source of inspiration becomes an ethical basic as well as a common obligation. In this revitalizing cry, we beseech perusers from all edges of the globe to add to the protection of Sumatran tigers, shielding an animal types as well as the rich biodiversity and sensitive biological systems that characterize Sumatra's rainforests.

1. **Grasping the Effect of Individual Commitments**
1. **The Force of Aggregate Activity:**
   It is fundamental to perceive that singular activities, when joined, employ colossal impact. An aggregate obligation to preservation rises above geographic limits, social contrasts, and financial inconsistencies. By encouraging a feeling of shared liability, every individual turns into a specialist of good change, adding to the conservation of Sumatran tigers and the biological systems they possess.
2. **Gradually expanding influences of Preservation Decisions:**

Each decision we make, from the items we buy to the energy we consume, meaningfully affects the climate. Cognizant choices to help reasonable practices, lessen our natural impression, and supporter for moral industrialism send a strong message. These singular decisions all in all enhance the effect on lessening territory obliteration, checking unlawful natural life exchange, and cultivating a worldwide protection ethos.

II. Supporting Protection Associations and Drives

1. **Monetary Commitments:**
   Direct help to respectable protection associations is a substantial and significant method for contributing. Monetary commitments, whether one-time gifts or normal participations, give fundamental assets to on-the-ground protection endeavors. These assets might be directed into territory assurance, hostile to poaching measures, local area commitment, and exploration drives — all fundamental parts of complete preservation systems.
2. **Sponsorship and Reception Projects:**

Taking part in sponsorship and reception programs presented by preservation associations is a customized road of help. Numerous associations give potential chances to emblematically embrace a Sumatran tiger, straightforwardly adding to its consideration, recovery, and delivery. Such projects not just proposition a more profound association with individual tigers yet in addition add to more extensive preservation objectives.

III. Support and Mindfulness Building

1. **Enhancing the Protection Message:**
   Tackling the force of backing and mindfulness building is vital in activating public help. People can become diplomats for Sumatran tiger protection by utilizing their interpersonal organizations, sharing data, and scattering legends encompassing tiger-related items. The intensification of the preservation message through computerized stages, public talking commitment, and local area outreach brings issues to light and cultivates a culture of empathy for untamed life.

2. **Participating in Advanced Activism:**

The computerized domain gives a strong field to activism. Using virtual entertainment stages, people can take part in and advance web-based crusades upholding for Sumatran tiger preservation. Petitions, hashtags, and viral difficulties can produce broad consideration, convincing legislatures and partnerships to focus on protection drives and establish strategy changes.

IV. Economical Customer Practices

1. **Moral Industrialism:**
   Embracing economical and moral purchaser rehearses addresses an immediate commitment to the preservation cause. Careful decisions in buying products, especially those connected to deforestation and untamed life double-dealing, can essentially affect market interest. By supporting eco-accommodating items, picking guaranteed feasible brands, and staying away from things connected to living space obliteration, shoppers assume a urgent part in driving market influences towards preservation adjusted rehearses.

2. **Capable The travel industry:**

For those lucky enough to visit Sumatra or other tiger natural surroundings, capable the travel industry rehearses are vital. Choosing eco-accommodating facilities, complying to moral natural life seeing rules, and supporting local area based the travel industry drives add to protection endeavors.

Mindful the travel industry cultivates an agreeable connection among guests and the climate, guaranteeing that the monetary advantages of the travel industry convert into substantial preservation results.

V. Instruction and Limit Building

1. **Putting resources into Ecological Training:**
   Schooling remains as a foundation for encouraging a preservation mentality. Supporting and partaking in natural training drives outfits people with the information and mindfulness expected to pursue informed decisions. Whether through school programs, local area studios, or online courses, putting resources into training enables people to become educated advocates for Sumatran tigers and biodiversity safeguarding.
2. **Limit Working in Neighborhood People group:**

Building the limit of neighborhood networks living in closeness to tiger natural surroundings is essential to supportable preservation. Adding to drives that give elective jobs, support schooling and medical services, and enable networks to effectively participate in preservation cultivates a cooperative methodology. Engaged people group become partners in the assurance of Sumatran tigers, guaranteeing that protection endeavors line up with neighborhood necessities and desires.

VI. Embracing Feasible Advancement Models

1. **Supporting Green Drives:**
   Feasible improvement models that focus on natural protection offer a diagram for what's to come. Pushing for and supporting green drives at nearby, public, and global levels guarantees that financial advancement lines up with biological trustworthiness. This might incorporate advancing environmentally friendly power, pushing for mindful land-use approaches, and supporting organizations focused on reasonable practices.
2. **Adjusting Monetary Development and Protection:**

Adding to the talk on offsetting financial development with protection goals is indispensable. Empowering states and organizations to take on strategies that focus on both monetary turn of events and ecological supportability encourages a comprehensive methodology. This backing lines up with the comprehension that drawn out financial security is complicatedly connected to the soundness of biological systems, including those holding onto Sumatran tigers.

VII. Cooperation and Systems administration

1. **Shaping Associations:**
   People can effectively look for valuable chances to shape associations with similar associations, local gatherings, and preservation drives.
   Cooperative endeavors intensify the effect of protection tries, encouraging an organization of help that rises above individual commitments. By manufacturing collusions, people become piece of a more extensive development devoted to the conservation of Sumatran tigers.

2. **Participating in Worldwide Joint effort:**

Worldwide difficulties request worldwide arrangements. People can effectively participate in worldwide joint efforts by supporting global protection arrangements, partaking in transboundary drives, and upholding for strategic endeavors that focus on biodiversity preservation. Adding to the worldwide discussion builds up the interconnected idea of ecological issues and the common obligation regarding shielding the world's normal legacy.

VIII. A Vow for What's to come

All in all, the source of inspiration for perusers to add to the preservation of Sumatran tigers and their rainforest living space isn't simply an allure — it is a vow for what's to come. It is a guarantee to be stewards of our planet, to advocate for the voiceless, and to guarantee that the tradition of Sumatran tigers stretches out past our time.

By perceiving the force of individual commitments, supporting preservation associations, taking part in backing, embracing feasible practices, and cultivating coordinated effort, every peruser turns into a watchman of Sumatran tigers. decisions today reverberation through time, forming the predetermination of these sublime animals and the environments they possess.

In this aggregate undertaking, let us stand joined in our obligation to a future where the rainforests of Sumatra reverberation with the dynamic thunders of Sumatran tigers — a future where the sensitive dance of biodiversity proceeds, stainless by the phantom of termination. The source of inspiration is a challenge to be important for this extraordinary excursion, an excursion that rises above limits, societies, and ages — an excursion toward a reality where the presence of Sumatran tigers isn't a unique case yet a demonstration of our common devotion to protection and the prospering life on The planet.